D0938471

NORWAY
AND THE SECOND
WORLD WAR

NORWAY
AND THE SECOND
WORLD WAR

BY

JOHS. ANDENÆS
Dr. juris

O. RISTE
D. Phil. (Oxon)
Editor

M. SKODVIN
Dr. philos.

ASCHEHOUG

© Johs. Andenæs, O. Riste, M. Skodvin. 1966
Fifth edition 1996
Printed in Norway
Engers Boktrykkeri A/S, Otta 1996
ISBN 82-03-22163-7

FOREWORD

The German invasion of Norway in 1940 opened a crucial chapter of Norwegian history. During the five years that followed, the fate of this nation on the outskirts of Europe was firmly interlocked with the gigantic struggle that raged in Europe and beyond. Yet Norway's war, while being a part of the universal conflict, still presented many unique features.

So far, the results of scholarly enquiry into this period of Norway's history have mostly been available only to those who read Norwegian. Consequently, people abroad who are interested in Norwegian war-time history have had to rely on the occasional, often inadequate and sometimes distorting, accounts that have been published abroad.

The present work is an attempt to amend this situation, by providing a balanced and concise survey of the period. But rather than presenting just a condensed review of Norwegian war-time history in all its aspects, the authors have chosen to emphasize the less accessible—and therefore more easily misunderstood—story of collaboration with the enemy during the occupation. To a large extent the authors have relied on their own study of the events, but the aim has also been to present a critical synthesis of years of conscientious research by a number of scholars.

The publication of this book is partly due to an initiative of the Press Department of the Royal Norwegian Ministry of Foreign Affairs. But the book is in no way an "official version" of history—nor, for that matter, does such a version exist. The three authors are solely and individually responsible for what they have written, and in particular for the views and conclusions put forward.

O. Riste

CONTENTS

THE POST-WAR PROCEEDINGS AGAINST
ENEMY COLLABORATORS (J. Andenæs)

War comes to Norway

NORWEGIAN NEUTRALITY

Upon the dissolution of the Union with Sweden in 1905, Norway became the master of its own foreign policy. From that moment, and until the German assault in the early hours of 9 April 1940, neutrality formed the firm and undisputed basis of that foreign policy. In fact, neutrality soon assumed almost the character of "an unwritten part of the Constitution, a state maxim unaffected by changing governments and parliaments"[1]. However, as times changed, and the conditions affecting Norway's place on the international scene altered accordingly, the policy of neutrality came to mean different things.

At the outset, the word "neutrality" and its popular catchphrase companion of "we want no foreign policy" shielded an almost exclusive concern with the country's internal affairs and problems. Freed from the strain and strife that marked the final years of the Swedish—Norwegian union, a new workingday was about to begin which required concentration of effort on creating an independent, prosperous and modern nation. What Norway desired from international politics was respect for its wish to be left alone—and there seemed to be no obvious reason why this desire should not be fulfilled.

Indeed, the experiences of the First World War, from which Norway emerged with a shaken economy but nevertheless relatively unscathed, appeared to confirm the wisdom of the chosen policy. The documentary evidence which could have shaken this confidence in Norwegian neutrality was buried in diplomatic archives both at home and abroad, and those who might have suspected that the country's position was more exposed than had been immediately apparent seemed ready to believe that the survival of neutrality was due to a combination of agile diplomacy and military preparedness.

1 *Stortingstidende* (parliamentary proceedings) 1920, 7a, col. 425.

9

After 1918, the departure from strict neutrality which Norway's membership in the League of Nations entailed was more formal than real. The widespread hope and idealism, which during the 1920s made Europe look to Geneva for a lasting assurance of peace among nations, was fully shared by the Norwegian people but was hardly accompanied by an adequate understanding of the obligations that membership of the League involved, even for small nations. Subsequently, economic difficulties of both national and international origin, as well as indigenous political problems, served to accentuate the people's preoccupation with the country's own affairs.

In the thirties, moreover, the increasingly evident disability of the League of Nations as a pacifying factor caused Norway and other small European nations gradually to withdraw from their already rather half-hearted commitment to the principles of collective security. However, the seemingly logical consequence of this withdrawal—a search for security at the national if not at the regional Scandinavian level—became submerged by the pressure of internal economic and social issues with their more immediately relevant concerns. Even those who accepted the principle that collective security had to be replaced by national security found it necessary in practice to compromise on the desirable level of defence preparedness, in view of other and conflicting demands on the national economy.

There was no lack of arguments to justify a relatively low priority for defence expenditure. War seemed a remote possibility, at least until the late thirties; and even if war came it would surely affect Norway only indirectly, because of the nation's determination to remain neutral as in the past. In the absence of evidence to the contrary, it was only natural to assume that Norwegian neutrality had not been seriously threatened at any time during the previous war. Hence, if there were any lesson to be learned from the past, it appeared to underline the truism that neutrality was a political rather than a military matter. From the experiences of 1914—1918 it could be assumed that neutrality also in the future would bring economic problems in its wake. Trade and shipping would inevitably be seriously affected. But from these assumptions to the expectation of more direct threats calling for active military measures was a long step, and a step which few were prepared to take.

Besides, from which direction could such threats be coming? From the Soviet Union? For centuries this eastern shadow had been a factor to be reckoned with in Scandinavian foreign policy. However, since the First World War the "eastern menace" had seemed a remote possibility in the military sphere. Many considered the political menace of communism to be infinitely more sinister, but from that angle it could well be argued that the best defence was to devote greater resources to the improvement of the social and economic conditions of the Norwegian people—not to build up military forces.

In regard to Germany as a potential aggressor, the evidence of the previous war was rather ambiguous. Memories of the crisis in the autumn of 1916, when diplomatic troubles between Norway and Germany caused by Norwegian trade restrictions and Germany's submarine warfare had seemed to carry the seeds of violent conflict, appeared to emphasise the danger from Germany. On the other hand, the comparative ease with which a political solution had then been found suggested either that the conflict was a sham or, at least, that it had been of a nature amenable to a solution on a strictly political level. Taking a longer view, the experiences of the First World War, and in particular the rather passive German acquiescence in the diminishing returns of Norwegian neutrality, appeared to demonstrate Norway's relative immunity to German pressure.

Beneath all this, of course, lay the fundamental assumption of Norwegian strategy: Britannia's rule of the waves, particularly the choppy waves of the North Sea. The disarmingly candid statement by Norway's Prime Minister in 1908 that "we trust in the British nation" had much truth in it then, but was far more directly applicable to the situation on the eve of the Second World War. In the face of British naval power, German forces would surely never be able to approach, let alone conquer, the Norwegian coast!

Finally, for the sake of completing this *tour d'horizon,* there was the eventuality of aggression from the Western Powers with the aim of converting neutral Norway into a reluctant ally. This, if at all conceivable, would most likely make whatever armed force Norway could muster against it not only useless, but positively dangerous; useless because it would in any case be utterly overwhelmed, dangerous because it might push Norway over into the opposite camp, against Norwegian sympathies and contrary to common and economic sense. If any "lesson of history" had undisputed validity, it would appear to be that Norway's vulnerable economy could never survive the enmity of Great Britain.

This wall of arguments for a neutrality that was only symbolically armed has both flaws and obvious weaknesses to a retrospective observer. But the attacks levelled against it at the time had little piercing effect, even if they succeeded in overcoming the initial, emotional reaction against anything that could possibly be construed as "war-mongering". Assertions about the duty of the neutral state to defend itself, about the danger that neutrality might be undermined through the cumulative effect of unopposed minor infringements, or about the temptation which a military vacuum constituted to a great power with an offensive strategy, could all be met with the admission that this called for neither more nor less than a certain minimum of military preparedness; and since this minimum was hard to define, it was tacitly assumed to be in the neighbourhood of the existing strength of Norway's defences.

Looking back, perhaps the fundamental weakness of the debate that went on during the 1930s was its disregard of the deeper significance of Norway's neutrality problems in the First World War. Both the familiar problems concerning Norwegian foreign trade and shipping, and some less familiar but more serious ones that were focused on the strategic value of Norwegian coastal waters—highlighted by the mine barrage across the North Sea—all served in the last resort to demonstrate Norway's potential importance in another conflict between Germany and Great Britain.

The two aspects of belligerency that seriously affected Norway in the First World War, Britain's blockade of Germany and Germany's submarine warfare, were bound to play important parts in a new conflict. But the fact that these were in essence weapons of economic warfare did not mean that they could be regarded in isolation, separate from over-all strategy. Both blockade and submarine warfare were economic in their purpose, but political and military in their methods. If a strategically exposed neutral state like Norway did not acquiesce in or co-operate with the efforts to intensify the impact of these weapons, then this was bound to raise the question whether the interests of belligerency would be better served by converting that neutral into an ally, however unwilling. And in the balance of that argument, the sanctity of neutrality could not be relied upon to have a decisive effect. The issue, in the glaring light of the necessities of war, was more likely to be whether the advantages of controlling Norway and its territory outweighed the benefits of a continued Norwegian neutrality. Then there were the political and military risks involved if force had to be used, and finally, in the context of 1939, the question of anticipating the enemy's next move.

With these terms of reference the position of each of the three countries immediately concerned on the eve of the war can better be understood. Reduced to the extreme, it may be said that Norway was prepared for the previous war, in that the Government expected to solve the questions of supplies, trade and shipping in the best possible way through political negotiations, relying on survival through neutrality even at a price.

The previous war also played an important part in the thinking behind German and British preparations, but at a different level. This was a different world and Norway was no longer outside the danger zone. In Germany, many believed that their largely passive naval strategy in the First World War had been a failure, and that the lack of imaginative pre-war planning had blunted even the offensive threat of submarine warfare. Could not this failure be remedied by a new German navy, better equipped with submarines, guided by less orthodox strategies and supported by air strength?

In Britain, on the other hand, the authorities studied the experiences of the blockade as it had developed during the First World War, not with a view to copying those experiences, but for the purpose of perfecting the system without repeating the gradual evolution and the many mistakes that had hampered its effectiveness. One way of achieving this where the neutrals were concerned was to supplement the traditional "blockade by agreement" with direct action, where British naval power could be brought to bear; and this is where the supply of Scandinavian iron ore to Germany entered the picture.

BRITAIN, FRANCE AND THE "IRON ROAD"
Initial Schemes

Winston Churchill, who on the outbreak of the war had become First Lord of the Admiralty with a seat in Chamberlain's War Cabinet, was acutely aware that the blockade was Britain's "principal naval offensive measure" and lost no time in trying to make full use of it. This awareness, combined with his predilection for flank strategy and his conviction that the Scandinavian peninsula had an "immense strategic significance"[1], led him as early as 19 September 1939 to propose action against the transport of Swedish iron ore from Narvik in North Norway to Germany. Churchill's idea was to lay a minefield across Norwegian territorial waters in order to force the ore transports out into the open sea where the British navy could deal with them. He at once instructed the Admiralty to examine the issue in detail while he himself tried to sell the scheme to his Cabinet colleagues. The question was however of no immediate urgency, and this as well as the political considerations involved caused the project to be put aside for the time being.

It was not until the second half of November that the issue of Scandinavian iron ore again appeared on the War Cabinet's agenda, but this time it had come to stay. The impetus now came from the Admiralty, which suggested the re-creation of the gigantic mine barrage of 1918 across the North Sea from the Orkneys to the Norwegian coast. Churchill put the proposal before the Cabinet, but since the time needed to carry out that project would not be less than six months he again advocated laying a smaller minefield in Norwegian waters at once.

[1] Churchill, *The Second World War*, Vol. I (Cassell, London, 1948), p. 420.

The Foreign Office remained doubtful about "the expediency as well as the legality of this plan"[1], but reports of an increasing ore traffic through Narvik convinced the Cabinet that the matter deserved a full examination from all angles. It was agreed that the chiefs of staff should present a report on the military problems involved, while the Ministry of Economic Warfare would study the economic aspects.

On the same day as the Cabinet called for these studies, however, Finland was attacked by the Soviet Union. This event placed the whole Scandinavian issue in a different light, and on Churchill's initiative the Foreign Office was asked to report on the political questions that might arise, particularly if a Russian attack on Norway and Sweden should extend the war to those countries. The three reports, together with a note from Churchill, were considered by the Military Co-ordination Committee on 20 December. The balance of the arguments about a minefield to hamper the Narvik ore traffic might well at this time have tipped in favour of action, under the added impetus of the German industrialist Thyssen's memorandum on the importance of Swedish ore which had been presented to the Supreme War Council by the French Prime Minister the day before. On the other hand, military considerations counselled caution in undertaking such action without having in readiness an expeditionary force that could be sent to neutralise the effects of a possible German retaliation. Moreover, the complications caused by the Russo-Finnish war tended to link up various alternative plans and contingencies in a rather intricate tangle.

At this point the French delegate to the Supreme War Council put forward a scheme which had the attractions of a purely diplomatic *démarche,* but at the same time held out the prospect of further action of the most far-reaching kind. The French wanted first to assure Sweden and Norway of the fullest Franco-British co-operation in anything that might assist Finland against the Soviet Union. Such co-operation, if accepted in principle, could then be exploited to send an Anglo-French expedi-

1 Woodward, *British Foreign Policy in the Second World War* (London, 1962), p. 19.

tionary force which would occupy Narvik and the Swedish ore-fields as part of the process".[1]

The result of the debates in the Military Co-ordination Committee and the Cabinet was a compromise. Those who shrank from the prospect of immediate naval action—as suggested by Churchill—carried the day with a proposal for a diplomatic approach on the lines of the French plan, but did not commit themselves to subsequent action beyond authorising the War Office to plan the despatch of a force to Narvik.

From what is known about the profusion of reports, studies and recommendations on the different aspects of the Scandinavian problem as seen by the Allies that winter, the "ifs and buts" and possible consequences involved still left wide open the question whether anything at all would follow the diplomatic overtures that were made. The unreal atmosphere is especially noticeable in the fundamental assumption about the consent of Norway and Sweden "to measures which would certainly involve these countries in the war against Germany"[2]—a remarkable instance of "wishful thinking which discounted the determination of the neutral Governments to maintain their neutrality"[3].

To Churchill the outcome of the December deliberations was a disappointment. Having at first welcomed the heightened interest in Scandinavian matters brought on by the question of assistance to Finland, since he thought it would help him to achieve "the major strategic advantage of cutting off the vital iron-ore supplies of Germany"[4], he now saw his cherished mining operation dropped on the pretext that it might "queer the pitch" of a major future operation in the same theatre. For the latter project Churchill had little enthusiasm. He did not believe the Scandinavians would consent to anything that would endanger their neutrality, and was concerned about the risk of an open conflict with the Soviet Union.

Meanwhile an *aide-mémoire* to the Norwegian and Swedish

---

[1] Butler, *Grand Strategy*, Vol. II (London, 1957), p. 100.
[2] Woodward, p. 21.
[3] Butler, p. 108.
[4] Churchill, p. 430.

Daladier, Chamberlain and Churchill, in a picture taken after the meeting of the Supreme War Council on 5 February 1940.

Governments had informed them of French and British intentions to give Finland indirect assistance, and of their willingness to co-operate with those Governments concerning such assistance as well as its "possible consequences". As the replies made it clear that Norway and Sweden had no desire even to discuss such co-operation, a second and more alarming *aide-mémoire* to Norway on 6 January 1940 stated that, on account of the recent torpedoing of Allied and neutral ships in Norwegian waters, the British felt obliged to extend their own naval operations into those waters.[1]

An emphatic protest from the Norwegian Government had the effect that the British Cabinet on 12 January decided that no action would be taken against the Narvik traffic "at present", although the pressure on Norway would be maintained. However, there still remained the plan for an expeditionary force to be landed with Scandinavian consent at an unspecified later

[1] Cf. Woodward, pp. 21—23.

date. Originally concerned only with Narvik, this plan had now been extended to include forces for the occupation of Stavanger, Bergen and Trondheim in the event of a German move towards southern Norway. Again, therefore, the larger project would seem to have prevailed over Churchill's "small plan", although Churchill believed there was "very little chance of the big plan being resolutely attempted".[1]

"The Big Plan"

Towards the end of January the military plans began to take shape on both sides of the Channel, and on 5 February the Supreme War Council, after disposing of an alternative French plan to approach the ore fields as well as Finland through the Petsamo area, agreed in principle to the "large project". In order to prevent the Germans from extracting the iron ore through the Baltic as soon as the ice broke up, the operation would have to start by approximately the middle of March. In all, and including forces to help the Swedes in resisting a German invasion, 100—150,000 troops would be involved in a move that was expected to take eleven weeks. So far, the Imperial General Staff had earmarked two territorial divisions and the 5th Regular Division for the purpose, in addition to a group being trained for winter warfare at Chamonix. The large scale of the enterprise caused some misgivings when the British Cabinet was asked to approve the plan, but the scheme went through —always on the assumption that the Scandinavian Governments would give their consent. Chamberlain thought that "refusal was unlikely, though we might get formal protests".[2]

Just before midnight on 16 February units of the British navy entered Norwegian territorial waters and boarded the German ship *Altmark* which was returning from service with the pocket-battleship *Graf Spee*. British sailors who had been held prisoner on board the *Altmark* were liberated, and Norwegian naval vessels nearby refrained from intervening against the superior

---

[1] Churchill, p. 438.

[2] Woodward, p. 25. On the military aspects of the plan, see i. a. Derry, *The Campaign in Norway* (London, 1952), p. 13, and (ed. Macleod and Kelly) *The Ironside Diaries 1937—1940* (London, 1962), p. 210.

The German ship "Altmark" in Jøssingfjord just after the events of 16 February. On deck are coffins of German sailors killed when the ship was boarded.

British force. The Norwegian Government issued an immediate and sharp protest against Britain's violation of neutral waters, to the accompaniment of Germany's serious warning about the possible effects of the incident. In Britain, however, the action was greeted with satisfaction, and considered a justifiable technical infringement in view of Norway's alleged failure to ensure universal respect for the sanctity of its maritime territory.

In the wake of this incident Churchill took the opportunity to urge once again the laying of a minefield in Norwegian waters. The moment was favourable: a lengthy discussion in the Cabinet led to an authorisation for "immediate naval preparations", and Churchill wasted no time in instructing the First Sea Lord to plan the operation which—"being minor and innocent, may be called 'Wilfred'"[1]. But Churchill was once more thwarted by legal and political considerations. Moreover,

[1] Churchill, pp. 598—99; Butler, pp. 111—12.

time now seemed to be running out on those who set greater store by the "larger plan". At the end of February, just when it was reported that the force destined for Stavanger, Bergen and Trondheim was now getting ready, the news from Finland strongly indicated that it might all be too late.

On 1 March the French and British Governments were approached from Finland with a series of questions about the possibility of assistance. The questionnaire seemed more intended to clear the way for negotiations with the Russians than as an actual appeal for help. Nevertheless, this prompted the Allies to inform Sweden and Norway that passage for forces to assist Finland would shortly be requested. The intimidation met with blank refusal on all points, and the Norwegian Government bluntly declared that it "did not wish to let itself be dragged into the European war and make Norway into a battlefield for a Great Power struggle".[1]

However, as in the following days signs were multiplying that the end of Finnish resistance was near, the French began to press for action which was meant to "test on the Norwegian beaches the firmness of the opposition"[2]. On 12 March the preparations for expedition "Avonmouth" were nearly complete, and two British brigades were assembled for embarkation on transport ships in the Clyde estuary. But the British Cabinet still stuck to its decision not to let the operation go ahead without a Finnish appeal for troops. Such an appeal never came. Instead, in the early hours of 13 March, the news reached London that the Russo-Finnish war had come to an end with Finland's acceptance of the Soviet terms.

The end of Finland's war removed the pretext for carrying out the large Anglo-French project in Scandinavia, and at a dejected meeting of the British Cabinet on 14 March the plan was cancelled.[3] Despite protests from the Chief of the Imperial General Staff, who wanted to keep the expeditionary force in being, the larger part of the British forces held ready now proceeded

[1] *UK Report, Appendices*, Vol. I, p. 222.

[2] Butler, p. 113. For "Avonmouth" cf. Kennedy, *The Business of War* (London, 1957), pp. 46—51.

[3] Cf. Butler, p. 113; Churchill, p. 453; Derry, p. 14. French reaction in Mordal, *La Campagne de Norvège* (Paris, 1949), p. 427.

to their original destination at the front in France, where they were anxiously awaited. The French Government, after some hesitation, released the shipping collected for the expedition, whereas the troops trained for winter warfare returned to their training grounds in the French Alps.

Final Allied Decisions.

The disappointment over the abandoned Scandinavian expedition was no doubt keenly felt by both Allies, but it was all the more bitter to those leading Frenchmen who had been most enthusiastic about the plan. Daladier's Cabinet fell on the issue, although Daladier remained as Defence Minister in the new Government. Both he and Admiral Darlan were reluctant to give up the idea of action in Scandinavia. A pretext had been lost, but the advantages of the operation remained the same. Moreover, the Russian-Finnish armistice had removed the danger of conflict with the Soviet Union which the British had feared.

For our purpose, the disappearance of the complications caused by the Finnish issue also had the important side-effect of bringing into clearer perspective the motives behind the Scandinavian plans—on both sides of the Channel—and it may be useful at this stage to set them out anew and more succinctly. To the French, the motives or in other words the advantages to be gained by operations in the north were three-fold. First, they offered the Allies an opportunity of seizing the initiative in a war whose "phoney" character was beginning to tell on the morale of the French people. Second, such operations would mean the opening of a diversionary theatre, far removed from the western front where the troops had spent a whole winter playing an agonising waiting game. Third, there were the supposedly decisive results to be achieved by a stoppage of the flow of Swedish iron ore to the German war industry.

To those in Britain who advocated action in Scandinavia, the iron ore was the main preoccupation. As in France, the stoppage of the iron route was judged to be of decisive importance, although the British seem to have had a somewhat clearer realisation that the Narvik route was not the whole problem. In assessing the motives on the British side, however, it is necessary to keep in mind the composition of the British Cabinet. In the main it was the same group of persons as had carried through the appeasement policy towards Germany, seeking to avoid a war or, at worst, to see it postponed until a time when the Allies were more ready to meet the German challenge. This was not a Cabinet prone to quick offensive decisions, daring initiatives or rash actions.

In this group, Churchill was an anomaly and an estranged element, reluctantly taken into the group in response to popular demand as the war broke out over Poland, but never really assimilated. Hence, whereas the Cabinet as a whole frequently hesitated and stuck to a cautious line, Churchill relentlessly bombarded them with schemes of varying soundness from his fertile brain. Churchill stood second to none in his estimate of the importance of blocking the iron route. Besides, he saw in this project an excellent chance of exerting his favourite weapon of British naval power. In so far as he needed any additional motives, the chance of gaining the initiative also found full favour with him, whereas the idea of a diversion away from the West European theatre of war played no part.

In regard to the wider context of operations in Scandinavia it is difficult, with the available material, to establish the opinion of Churchill and those who supported his views—such as General Ironside, Chief of the Imperial General Staff. It is open to debate whether Churchill really believed that a large-scale German reaction would follow in the wake of mine-laying in Norwegian waters. In a sense, however, the question to him may have been unimportant: if it did not have such consequences, the primary purpose of the minefield would still be fulfilled, and if it did lead to a German invasion he had no fear that the Allies—and the British navy in particular—would not be able to nullify whatever advantages the Germans hoped to gain from such action. In fact, Churchill thought such events would turn to the advantage of the Allies. The issue in his mind, therefore, was a simple one. The British should lay the minefield, and in case the Germans were rash enough to retaliate, a force would be held ready to answer the challenge and secure the full advantages of an Allied hold on Scandinavia.

After 12 March, and now freed from the complications of a possible conflict with the Soviet Union over Scandinavia, Churchill resumed his efforts in favour of action against the Narvik route. At a Cabinet meeting on 18 March he mentioned that a plan was being examined by his naval staff.[1] Another plan which Churchill enthusiastically promoted was the so-called "Royal Marine" operation of sowing mines in the Rhine in order to create havoc in German transports on that important waterway. During a visit to France in the middle of March he sought to overcome French fears that actions so near to the western front would provoke an immediate retaliation against French territory.

The French, however, remained firm adherents of diversions in other and more peripheral theatres.[2] At a meeting of French commanders-in-chief on 15 March, Darlan reverted to the question of Scandinavia from the view-point of the iron ore, and suggested an ultimatum to Norway and Sweden demanding the cessation of further exports of that commodity to Germany. This, he thought, would almost certainly provoke a German reaction whatever answer Sweden and Norway gave—a reaction which would permit the Allies to resume their project and open the northern theatre of operations. On the same day Daladier, in an *aide-mémoire* to the British Government, stressed the need to assume effective control of Norwegian waters, completed if necessary by the occupation of a base on land.

Paul Reynaud, who took over as Premier after Daladier's Cabinet fell on the Finnish issue, also saw in *"la bataille du fer"* the best solution to the Allies' two fundamental problems—the physical one of cutting off Germany's essential supplies, and the equally important psychological one of seizing the initiative in the war and thereby gaining the confidence of the neutrals in a final victory for the Allies. Above all, as stressed in a French memorandum dated 25 March, it must not be assumed that

---

1 Medlicott, *The Economic Blockade*, Vol. I (London, 1952), pp. 191—92.

2 Cf. Mordal, pp. 109—112; Reynaud, *La France a sauvé l'Europe*, Vol. II (Paris 1947), p. 26; Gamelin, *Servir*, Vol. III (Paris, 1947), p. 215.

time was on the side of Britain and France. With this last point the British chiefs of staff—in an interim appreciation of the military situation—agreed, to the extent that time was on the side of the Allies only if they took the fullest possible advantage of it. The way to do it was not, however, to adopt "spectacular but unsound projects"[1], but to intensify the building up of resources in preparation for a general offensive strategy. The Foreign Office took a similar line and preferred a direct blow at Germany by means of the "Royal Marine" operation.

In this mood the Allied war leaders prepared for the scheduled meeting of the Supreme War Council in London on 28 March. Britain's preferred policy in Scandinavia was indicated in the Cabinet's decision, on the eve of the meeting, to warn the Scandinavian Governments that the Allies could not tolerate policies that gave unequal advantages to Germany. They would therefore reserve their right to take the necessary measures to prevent such assistance to Germany's warfare[2]. It was left to the Supreme War Council to decide what action could be taken, but the pattern of opinions was already apparent in the preliminary meeting of the military chiefs. The French wanted to land, whereas the British wanted to restrict themselves to mine-laying.

The meeting[3] of the Supreme War Council was opened by Chamberlain with a lengthy survey in which he outlined Britain's suggestions for the conduct of the war. At the head of the list, to Churchill's great satisfaction, was the "Royal Marine" operation. After that came the issue of Germany's "two weaknesses: her supplies of iron ore and of oil". The Prime Minister pointed out the vulnerability of the sea routes for the iron ore transport from Narvik and Luleå to Germany, and put to the Council the Cabinet's decision of the previous day, about a diplomatic approach which left open the opportunity for practical measures. Finally, regarding Germany's supply of Rumanian oil, he concluded in favour of actions that were purely diplomatic. Reynaud, in his statement, referred to the general feeling

1 Butler, p. 120.

2 *Ibid.*, p. 121.

3 Cf. Butler, p. 121; Churchill, pp. 455–57; Woodward, p. 31; Gamelin, pp. 297–98; Mordal, pp. 117–20.

in France that the war had reached a deadlock, and that resolute action was necessary. He thought that "Royal Marine", whatever its merits, was only a temporary expedient, and expected far more from cutting off the supplies to Germany of Swedish iron ore, first by mine-laying along the Norwegian coast, later by similar action against the Luleå traffic.

From Reynaud's statement it was fairly obvious that French acceptance of "Royal Marine" could only be expected as the result of some "*quid pro quo*" arrangement, and the outcome of the deliberations was a decision for action both in Scandinavia and on the Rhine. The Allies would address a diplomatic note to Norway and Sweden on the first or second day of April along the lines already approved by the British Cabinet. This was to be followed on 5 April by the laying of mines in Norwegian territorial waters. Operation Royal Marine would be executed in two stages on 4 and 15 April—subject to the French War Committee's approval which presumably was regarded as a mere formality.

So far everything seemed clear-cut, although there loomed in the minds of at least some of those present the question of what consequences the mine-laying in Norwegian waters might have. The French seem to have expected a German retaliation, and welcomed the prospect. The British, on balance, do not seem to have believed that the mine-laying would by itself cause Germany to invade Norway, but on 29 March the War Cabinet decided, in view of the possibility of a violent German reaction, to prepare a military expedition for the moment when "the Germans set foot on Norwegian soil, or there is clear evidence that they intend to do so".[1]

In retrospect, this "moment" of action seems both too vague and too late. But the vagueness must be seen in connection with the political necessity to wait until clear evidence about a German assault could remove Norwegian suspicions about the motives for Britain's action. The Allied directives also contained instructions to the effect that no landings would take place "if the Norwegians were hostile". The lateness of the defined "moment" seems clearly connected with the prevalent under-

1) Derry, p. 15; Butler, p. 123. Cf. also Woodward, p. 31.

estimation of Germany's capacity to strike quickly and hard in Norway: the British doubted Germany's ability to forestall them at Bergen and Trondheim, and never even considered the possibility of this happening at Narvik.

The question now arose of finding the forces for this military expedition. On the British side, the mainstay of the large plan from February was no longer available, as the skiers of the 5th Scots Guards had been disbanded and the 41st and 44th Divisons had been sent to France. The 5th Regular Division which acted as a reserve for the "large plan" had never left France and could not now be extricated from its position on the line. There remained the incomplete 49th Division and the 24th (Guards) Brigade, and these were now alerted. It was decided that the Guards would be earmarked for Narvik, to be sent by transport, while the territorial troops would be distributed with one battalion for Trondheim—also in a transport—and four battalions to go by cruiser to Stavanger and Bergen. The troops were to be ready for departure almost immediately after the minefields had been laid, and would act in accordance with a hastily revised version of the directives for the corresponding part of the abandoned "large plan".[1]

During these early days of April, however, it appears to have been the turn of the French to cause the lion's share of confusion and hesitation. On 1 April the British Cabinet was told that the approval of the French War Committee for operation "Royal Marine", thought to be a mere formality, was not forthcoming for at least three months. The British now at first decided to withhold the notes prepared for the Swedish and Norwegian Governments, but three days later the delivery date was set for 5 April, to be followed by mine-laying on 8 April. Neither General Ironside, on 4 april, nor Chamberlain the next day, now expected any major German retaliation to the mine-laying. Reports did suggest, however, that something was being prepared in Germany.[2] What could it be?

[1] Cf. Derry, pp. 15—16; Butler, p. 124 and Ash, *Norway 1940* (London, 1964), pp. 24—25. Also British regimental histories (see bibliography).

[2] Mordal, p. 130; Butler, p. 123; Churchill, p. 459; Roskill, *The War at Sea*, Vol. I (London, 1954), p. 158.

The only serious encounter between the German invasion fleet on its way to Norway and the British Navy: HMS "Glowworm" being pursued by the German cruiser "Hipper".

Postscript on Decision-Making

One recurrent problem in the study of Allied planning for Scandinavia, arises from the British method of "waging war by committee". This method meant that however advanced the military and operational plans may have been at any given moment, all plans as well as more concrete preparations were at any time subject to instant revision or cancellation by the political authorities, – at any time, that is, until the forces were actually in action. Moreover, even beyond that point the machinery could be stalled, by means of the built-in political reservations which, as we have seen, meant a severe limitation on the freedom of action of the forces concerned.

On Germany's side, too, there existed the same reservations about sudden cancellation of military plans. However, this was to a large extent obviated by the fact that Hitler held

27

the reins of both political and military leadership in his own hands. Therefore, political consent was to a much greater degree involved as the Führer, at each major cross-roads beyond the level of purely intellectual staff exercises in planning, gave his authorisation for the next stage of the process to begin. The German "establishment" was seldom so solid and unanimous behind each new war move as many are inclined to believe. Rivalries and military opposition occurred. But political remorse played little or no part in the process. Sudden, last-minute repeal of a planned operation was hence not likely to be caused by political second thoughts, but rather by reasons of a military nature beyond Germany's control.

THE GERMAN PLANS

The Development of an Idea

At the time of the outbreak of the First World War, Germany's naval strategy was essentially defensive in character. Its salient feature was that the "High Seas Fleet", belying its name, would play the part of a "fleet in being" for the purpose of deterring the enemy from offensive operations in the vicinity of German territory. Post-war critics of this strategy, of whom the most prominent was Vice-Admiral Wolfgang Wegener, considered it to have been a complete failure and a waste of naval power, as it meant defending positions which were in fact never attacked. Moreover, the severe restrictions thus laid upon the fleet facilitated the enemy's establishment of a distant but watertight blockade ring around the Central Powers. Against this development the only offensive weapon available to the German navy had been the submarines, and however effective these had at times shown themselves to be, their full potential could only be realised under a different and offensive general strategy which aimed, *inter alia*, at providing operational submarine bases nearer to their hunting grounds in the Atlantic.

In the late 1930s, as German naval strategists faced the possibility of war against the superior British navy, the far-reaching implications of Wegener's criticism were by no means univer-

Grossadmiral Erich Raeder.

sally accepted. But at least some of his ideas had caught the imagination of both Admiral Carls, Naval Commander in the Baltic, and *Grossadmiral* Raeder, Supreme Commander of the German navy. Before the war both men had been considering the desirability of forward bases in the north in a future conflict with Britain. Then, at the end of September 1939, when the *Blitzkrieg* campaign in Poland was practically over, Admiral Carls, according to Raeder's later testimony,[1] again took up the issue with his chief. At a subsequent meeting in the *Seekriegsleitung* (Naval War Staff) on 3 October, Raeder brought up for discussion the topic of naval bases in Norway and it was decided, as recorded in the war diary of the Naval Staff, that Raeder should inform Hitler of the considerations of the navy. In particular, the Naval Staff recommended an investigation of the possibility of a joint Russo-German pressure on Norway in order to obtain bases, for the purpose of "a fundamental improvement in our strategic and operational

1 IMT, Vol. 14. p. 86.

situation". Among the questions that required further study was: "Can the acquisition of the bases, insofar as it is impossible without the use of force, be achieved by the force of arms against Norway's will?".[1]

A few days after the discussion in the Naval War Staff the German submarine chief, Admiral Dönitz, submitted a memorandum on the issue from the viewpoint of submarine warfare. After enumerating the three essential prerequisites for a base in Norway, namely that it should be an ice-free port, accessible by rail and situated outside the narrow passage between Norway and the Shetlands, he limited the choice to Narvik and Trondheim. From a further consideration of their respective merits and drawbacks, Dönitz concluded that Trondheim ought to be established as a base for the supply and repair of submarines, whereas Narvik could serve as an auxiliary fuel supply station.[2]

In response to the questions raised at the conference on 3 October, the Naval Staff six days later presented a paper on the problems involved. While agreeing with Dönitz about the choice of Trondheim as the most suitable port, this document pointed to the complications that would arise if the base had to be acquired by the use of force. Although an initial *coup-de-main* operation might be successful in seizing the port, a continued resistance from Norway would almost certainly sever connections between Germany and the base. Moreover, the Chief of Staff, Admiral Schniewind, minuted to the memorandum that a *coup-de-main* operation would not be sufficient for the purpose. The base concerned could only be seized by means of a considerable force.[3]

Thus, although there was a clear realisation of the value of a base such as Trondheim for Germany's naval warfare, the Naval Staff showed a high degree of scepticism when it came to the question of seizing and holding the port against opposition. Raeder, however, was not discouraged, and took the opportunity of putting the issue to Hitler at a conference on naval affairs on 10 October. After opening remarks about the negli-

---

[1] IMT, Vol, 34, pp. 423–4, Doc. 122–C.

[2] IMT, Vol. 34, pp. 159–61, Doc. 005–C.

[3] Cf. Gemzell, *Raeder, Hitler und Skandinavien* (Lund, 1965), pp. 220–22.

gible value of a conquest of the Belgian coast from the viewpoint of submarine warfare, he pointed out to the Führer the usefulness of a base in Norway—notably Trondheim—which might be obtained with the aid of Russian pressure. Raeder's contemporary report of the meeting states that Hitler would "consider this matter".[1] Since it is known that Hitler was fully aware of the importance of submarine warfare from forward bases in the case of a prolonged war, his lack of interest in Raeder's suggestion indicates that his mind at this stage was occupied with the idea of a short war based on a rapid offensive in the west.

On the face of it, Raeder could also draw little comfort from the views of the Chief of the General Staff, Halder. At a conference with Schniewind early in October, Halder rejected out of hand the idea of a military operation to seize naval bases in Norway. His main reasons were the difficult terrain and the exposed lines of communications and supply which operations in Norway would involve. At the same time, Halder could not promise to provide the navy with a sufficiently wide basis in north-west France from which the submarines could operate. Raeder took note of the latter point, which effectively disposed of the value of the western offensive for the purposes of naval warfare. Halder's rejection of operations in Norway, however, was counteracted by an optimistic estimate of the possibilities from General Jodl, Chief of Operations in OKW *(Oberkommando der Wehrmacht)*, Hitler's Supreme Command.[2]

A reconstruction, at this stage, of Raeder's motives for persisting in his designs concerning the coast of Norway, would bring forth the following points. First, the prospect of a short war, with its inevitable emphasis on land warfare in a western offensive, would in itself be anathema to the navy. Not only would such a campaign put the navy low on the list of priorities for manpower and equipment; it would also offer little or no improvement in the navy's strategic position. At least from a narrow service viewpoint, therefore, a longer war in which Great

1 IMT, Vol. 35, p. 629, Doc. 879—D. Also *Brassey's Naval Annual, 1948* (London, 1948), p. 47.

2 Cf. Gemzell, pp. 226—27.

Britain could be identified as the main enemy would appear as the navy's real challenge. And in that context the Norwegian idea would come into its own. Not only would an action in Scandinavia by itself require a major naval effort, but bases on the coast of Norway would prepare the navy for a really decisive role in what Raeder had referred to as the "maritime siege of England".

For the time being, however, Raeder had to bide his time, although various staff studies of that autumn on matters concerning the navy and Scandinavia indicate that his interest had not diminished. Not before 25 November was the topic again raised at a conference of the Naval War Staff, and this time from a different angle. Raeder now pointed to the danger that the British, as a counter-stroke to German action against the Netherlands, might carry out a surprise landing in Norway and seize a naval base, and he ordered the Staff to prepare a study of this eventuality.[1]

This sudden mention of possible British designs on Norway, if seen against the background of what is now known about Churchill's active interest in Norway's strategic position, has often been connected with Raeder's later allegations that his Norwegian scheme was prompted by intelligence reports of impending Allied action in Norway. However, in the absence of documentary evidence to support these allegations, it seems more appropriate to conclude that Raeder was only drawing the consequence of the theoretical—but quite logical—assumption that the British might also in certain circumstances desire bases on the coast of Norway. What is at first sight more puzzling is that this realisation should come so late. But the prevailing view in Germany expected Britain and France to pursue a mainly passive "phoney war" role until their economic and military resources would permit an energetic struggle leading to a decisive victory. Conversely, of course, this view stressed the need for Germany to exploit this opportunity by securing the best starting positions for that struggle.

Apart from considerations of naval strategy, Raeder in this period also devoted attention to questions of economic warfare.

[1] Gemzell, p. 246.

Although such matters were the direct concern of Hitler's Supreme Command, Raeder saw the navy and especially the submarines playing an increasingly important part in this field. A greater emphasis on economic warfare would also serve the navy's interests by pointing to Britain as the main enemy. At a naval affairs conference with the Führer on 8 December, Raeder therefore brought up the question of Scandinavia from the angle of economic warfare. He drew Hitler's attention to the voluminous trade between Scandinavia and England—much of it passing through Trondheim but leaving Norwegian waters from so many scattered points on the coast that control was exceedingly difficult. This, according to the contemporary report of the conference in the naval war archives,[1] showed the importance of an occupation of Norway, whereby the exports from Scandinavia could moreover be deflected from Britain to Germany.

The absence of any recorded reaction from the Führer to this hint suggests that he still refused to take an active interest in Raeder's Norwegian schemes. However, Raeder was soon to receive support for his idea from quite different quarters, as two days later a Norwegian ex-Minister of Defence arrived in Berlin.

Quisling in Berlin.

Vidkun Quisling, a major in the Norwegian army, had been Minister of Defence for about two quarrelsome years when the Agrarian Government of which he was a member was forced to resign. Shortly thereafter, in May 1933, he founded a political party called *"Nasjonal Samling"*—National Unification. Its programme was fascist-inspired, and the party's conspicuous failure in the following years to assert itself within the framework of Norwegian parliamentary democracy seemed to leave it only the alternatives of either complete extinction or a precarious existence as a rightist lunatic fringe of Norwegian politics.

As early as 1930 Quisling had sought contact with German Nazis, but, in spite of intermittent relations through the thirties

1 Brassey, pp. 61–63.

with individual representatives of the German Nazi hierarchy, Quisling and his movement seemed to attract little interest. Not before the summer of 1939 did his connections begin to show some promise, and then it was the entourage of the Nazi ideologist Alfred Rosenberg who in their "greater Germanic" and "Nordic" enthusiasm began to take a more active interest in Quisling and his followers. During a visit to Germany in June 1939 Vidkun Quisling met Rosenberg in Berlin, and in the following autumn "Nasjonal Samling"—commonly referred to by its initials NS—remained in contact with Rosenberg's organisation through the Norwegian businessman Hagelin, who lived in Dresden.[1]

The next time Quisling met Rosenberg, in December 1939, the auspices were more favourable,—for one thing Scandinavia had now been drawn into the focus of great power politics through the Russian attack on Finland. From such contemporary evidence as the archives of the German Naval Staff and the diaries of General Jodl, chief of operations in Hitler's Supreme Command, and of Rosenberg himself, historians are able to establish a fairly clear picture of what happened during Quisling's visit to Berlin.

Quisling arrived in the evening of 10 December and was received the following morning by Rosenberg. During this first conversation, Quisling alleged that the pro-British circles in Norway under "the Jew Hambro" (C. J. Hambro was President of the Storting) were now intensifying their efforts against Germany. He then, in Rosenberg's words, "again put forward concrete proposal for preparing a German landing at the request of a new Government that would be set up".[2]

While Rosenberg thereafter went to inform Hitler of Quisling's arrival, Quisling and Hagelin at noon appeared for a meeting with Admiral Raeder. The record of this conference reports Quisling as having stated to Raeder that England would not in the long run respect Norwegian neutrality, and that there already existed a secret agreement between the British

[1] Cf. Skodvin, *Kampen om okkupasjonsstyret i Norge* (Oslo, 1956) pp. 22—29.

[2] (ed. Seraphim), *Das politische Tagebuch Alfred Rosenbergs* (DTV, München, 1964), pp. 110—11.

and Norwegian Governments. According to this alleged agreement, in the case of war between Norway and a great power, the English would be permitted to land near Stavanger and establish a base at Kristiansand. Quisling thereupon stressed the danger to Germany from such developments, and proceeded to explain the role he and his followers could play in that connection: "The national party wished to forestall such an English step, by putting corresponding bases at the disposal of German forces. There were already men in important positions (railways, mail, intelligence) in coastal areas that had been engaged for the cause."[1] Quisling's proposal was linked with his claim that, because the Norwegian Parliament had recently prolonged the period between elections from three to four years—a decision which in Quisling's view was unconstitutional, both the Storting and the Government would hold power illegally after 10 January 1940. This would offer possibilities of political upheaval, during which the "national party would step forward. Talks were therefore desirable about common action, transfer of troops to Oslo, etc."

Raeder's only recorded reaction to these ideas was a promise to bring the matter to the Führer's attention and to inform Quisling of the results. To Rosenberg, on the other hand, the Admiral described Quisling's arrival on the scene as "a gesture from destiny".[2]

On the following day, 12 December, Raeder had a meeting with the Naval Staff where Quisling's ideas and the Norwegian problem were discussed, after which he went to Hitler for another of his frequent top-level conferences on the naval situation. Present at this meeting were also General Keitel, together with General Jodl and Hitler's naval *aide-de-camp* von Puttkamer. The conference report[3] shows the Norwegian problem to have been the dominant topic, with Raeder reporting on Quisling's statements of the day before. His own comments were to the effect that Quisling appeared to be a reliable person, although caution was needed, since it was always difficult with such

1 Brassey, pp. 65—66.
2 Gemzell, p. 271; Skodvin, p. 31.
3 IMT, Vol. 34, pp. 271—73, Doc. 064—C; Brassey, pp. 66—67.

offers of co-operation to know how far the persons concerned were pushing their own interests or to what extent they had Germany's interests at heart. On the other hand, for Norway to fall into the hands of Britain might be decisive for the whole war. Raeder saw one drawback in a possible German seizure of bases on the Norwegian coast: it was bound to provoke strong British countermeasures against ore transports from Narvik, and this might in the long run be too tough a challenge for the German navy.

Raeder's proposal, to which the Führer gave his provisional approval, was to allow the OKW to concert plans with Quisling for the preparation and execution of an occupation of Norway, either by peaceful means—i. e. German forces called in by Norway, or by force. Jodl's diary expressed this proposition in the following terms: "Two cases, what happens when we are called in, what do we do if we have to gain a foothold by force? OKW shall work out study, in contact with previous Defence Minister."[1] In the afternoon Hitler decided to have another talk with Rosenberg before making up his mind whether he should see Quisling personally.

Rosenberg then went to Hitler, and returned home in the evening to have another long conversation with Quisling. That night he hit his previously injured foot against a door and was immobilised, so the result of his talk with Quisling had to be communicated to Raeder by post the following morning. This letter discussed whether to recommend Quisling for an audience with the Führer, and, although Rosenberg respectfully deferred to Raeder's expertise concerning the possibilities of action in Scandinavia, he added as his personal impression that "one must act when *can* act".[2] An enclosed memorandum gave, *inter alia,* further details of Quisling's "credentials", particularly his relationship with the Norwegian army, as Hitler had expressed some concern on that point. On 14 December Raeder visited Rosenberg at home, and they both agreed according to Rosenberg's diary "on the risk as well as on the necessity of

[1] (ed. Hubatsch), Jodl's diary for October 1939—January 1940 in *Die Welt als Geschichte* (Stuttgart) 1952, pp. 274—287 and 1953, pp. 58—71.
[2] Quisling Trial *(Straffesak mot V. A. L. J. Quisling,* Oslo, 1946), p. 47.

the action". Thereupon Raeder, together with Scheidt, Rosenberg's assistant, took Quisling and Hagelin to see the Führer. The outcome of Quisling's meeting with Hitler is concisely reported in Jodl's diary in the following form:

"Führer confers with Norwegian ex-Minister of Defence. 17.00 Führer commands investigation with the smallest of staffs on how the occupation of Norway can be carried out. 18.15 corresponding order from me to Captain von Sternburg."

In Rosenberg's diary appears a much more detailed account of the conference, evidently based on what Quisling, Hagelin and Scheidt reported to him the same evening. According to this source, Hitler in his opening monologue had said that he preferred Norway to remain neutral, but could on the other hand never permit the English to get hold of Narvik. After reading through a memorandum which Quisling had handed to him concerning the need for Greater Germanic unity, Hitler then listened as Quisling explained the Norwegian situation to him.

Quisling returned from his first meeting with Hitler feeling "very satisfield", and before leaving Berlin he had another audience with the Führer on 18 December during which he was finally assured that help from Germany would be forthcoming. At other meetings Quisling also met representatives of the Foreign Ministry and the Naval Staff, and Hitler's *aide-de-camp* Colonel Schmundt. Quisling left Berlin on 20 December, and Rosenberg, who was already looking forward to visiting Norway with Quisling as its *"Ministerpresident"*, could write in his diary that "the first stage of the planned Norwegian enterprise is completed".

"Studie Nord"

The scheme elaborated during Quisling's talks in Berlin can for purpose of simplicity be called "the political plan", or in Raeder's phraseology a plan for the occupation of Norway "by peaceful means, i. e. German forces called in by Norway." Its details can be studied in a portfolio which Rosenberg's *Aussenpolitisches Amt* (Foreign Policy Bureau), where the main responsibility for this alternative rested, transmitted to the Reich Chancellery for Hitler's information. A central document is the memorandum, already referred to, which Rosenberg wrote after his evening talk with Quisling and enclosed with his letter to Raeder the following morning.

According to this memorandum[1], a first stage in his and Quisling's plan would be to send selected Norwegians to Germany, where they could be trained for special tasks by experienced German Nazis. On their return to Norway they would then be available for actions such as shock seizures of communication centres, etc. Timed with a *coup d'état* units of the German navy with troops on board would be posted at selected points near the approaches to Oslo, ready to be called in by the new Norwegian Government. Quisling had no doubt that he would have the co-operation of his army connections in Norway once the initial coup had been successfully carried out.

In another document[2], based on the talks between Quisling and various German officials, mention is made of some specific problems that such an action might meet. The paper makes no secret of the fact that the overwhelming majority of Norwegians would assume an unfriendly attitude, and therefore stresses the need for continuous German support and an early police penetration of the country in order to forestall internal struggle. The necessity of careful political preparations, involving Rosenberg's organisation and the Reich Chancellery but bypassing the Foreign Ministry, is finally emphasised.

Rosenberg, it may be assumed, believed in this plan, since he sent his faithful assistant Scheidt back to Oslo with Quisling. However, the mere presence of a forceful alternative in Raeder's proposals to Hitler implies a mental reservation about Quisling's scheme in more responsible quarters, a reservation which was to be accentuated in the following weeks. Early in January Hitler gave expression to his growing scepticism, especially, if Rosenberg can be relied upon at this point, as regards the discretion of the Norwegians. German military leaders were even more negative towards the political plan, while work proceeded on *Studie Nord* as the forcible alternative. Towards the middle of January the initial OKW study was finished; it was passed to

---

1 IMT, Vol. 34, pp. 273–75, Doc. 065–C; Brassey, pp. 63–65.
2 Rosenberg, pp. 195–96.

the service staffs for comments, but was soon withdrawn as Hitler had decided to keep all the staff work within the frame of the OKW. Then, on 27 January, General Keitel issued an order from Hitler for the formation of a special staff in the OKW charged with preparing operational plans for what was thereafter to be known as *Weserübung*. In order to ensure Hitler's direct influence on the planning, the staff would be under Keitel's personal orders, and it was intended that this would later become the nucleus of an operational staff.[1]

With this decision, German planning for action in Norway had reached, and passed, another turning-point. We have previously indicated Quisling's visit to Berlin as decisive in bringing about a transition from the first stage — the development of an idea, namely Raeder's idea of acquiring naval bases in Norway —to the second stage of a staff study of this idea and the operations involved. With Hitler's decision on 27 January, and the inception of operational planning, the process entered its third stage. The special staff assembled on 5 February, and in conditions of utmost secrecy the elaboration of detailed plans could then begin.

Without carrying too far the speculation about Hitler's motive for allowing this third stage of planning for Norway to begin, it is worth noting that 20 January was the last in a long series of postponed "D-days" for the offensive against France. From then until the invasion actually started in May, no further alarms were called on Germany's western front. And each delay of Germany's *Blitzkrieg* in the west brought nearer the alternative—a longer war, with Britain as the main enemy and a siege of the British Isles in the air and under water as the way to victory. In addition, although the Germans had no knowledge of the plans being prepared in London and Paris, the Allied "public diplomacy" conducted around recent incidents in neutral Norwegian waters, and other available intelligence about Anglo-French pressure on Scandinavia, were sufficient to engender speculation about possible Allied designs on Norway.

1 Cf. Jodl Diary; Halder, *Kriegstagebuch,* Vol. I (Stuttgart, 1962), pp. 149—50; IMT, Vol. 34, pp. 181—85, Doc. 021—C and p. 270, Doc. 063—C. Also Hubatsch, *Weserübung* (Göttingen, 1960), pp. 31—32 and 356—57.

To all appearances it was the *Altmark* affair, mentioned above, which gave a real sense of urgency to the planning for *Weserübung*. Immediately thereafter, in what may well have been a mixture of acute realisation of the strategic significance of Norwegian waters and anger at the impertinence of the British naval action, Hitler gave orders for the plans to be accelerated. On 21 February General Niklaus von Falkenhorst, who had served in Finland in 1918 and therefore might have some relevant experience of operations in Scandinavia, was called to Hitler and put in charge of *Weserübung* preparations— which henceforth also included the occupation of Denmark.[1]

At the same time, the *Altmark* affair meant the *coup-de-grâce* to the political plan conceived by Rosenberg and Quisling. After a conversation with the Führer on 19 February, Rosenberg wrote in his diary that "hence falls... the political plan of the Norwegians. They must remain at our disposal in the event of our being forced to protect the access to Norway against British strangulation". Presumably for the latter purpose, but also in view of existing commitments through Scheidt's presence in Oslo and the financial support which had been given, Rosenberg some days later obtained Hitler's consent to increased subsidies for Quisling's movement.[2] But the Führer at the same time rejected sharply any suggestions of a political action originating from Norway.

On 23 February *Weserübung* was the topic of a conference between Hitler and Raeder.[3] The Führer now voiced his concern about the iron ore from Sweden, and Raeder admitted that the preservation of Norwegian neutrality offered the most favourable conditions in that respect. A German invasion of Norway would cause a temporary halt in the supplies that came via Narvik. However, even if this meant the loss of two or three million tons of ore a year, the sure prospect of the

---

[1] IMT, Vol. 28, p. 406, Doc. 1809—PS; Halder, p. 204.
[2] Rosenberg, pp. 123—24.
[3] Brassey, pp. 81—82.

complete stoppage of all Swedish ore supplies under a British occupation of Norway was infinitely more serious.

Towards the end of Febuary 1940 the preparations for *Weserübung* were sufficiently advanced for Jodl to suggest that this operation and the projected western offensive should be independent of each other, both in regard to timing and allotment of resources. On 1 March Hitler then issued his official directive for the occupation of Norway and Denmark. The motive for the operation, according to this document, was three-pronged: first, the need to forestall British action in Scandinavia and the Baltic, second, to secure the Swedish iron ore for Germany, and, finally, to improve the starting position of Germany's naval and air forces against Great Britain. The directive emphasised the desire to give the operation a peaceful character, but made it clear that any resistance must be broken by all available military means.

The actual operational orders for the action were drawn up after a top-level military conference on 5 March.[1] In its main features, the invasion of Norway would consist of three "waves" of troops, with respectively three, two and one divisions. Landings were foreseen simultaneously at seven different points on the coast from Oslo to Narvik, and the invasion troops would go partly in transport ships, partly—for the main onslaught—in warships. Cargo steamers with equipment and supplies were to leave Germany in time to be waiting for the troops at their ports of debarkation. The scale of the operation meant that practically the whole of the German navy would be involved, and the hazardous nature of the undertaking was stressed by the fact that, although the all-important conditions of secrecy and surprise might be achieved for the initial landings, the really dangerous part for the navy would be their subsequent return to German ports. That the German navy could with any measure of equanimity envisage such risks, is explained by the important role which the *Luftwaffe* would have to play in *Weserübung*. German superiority in the air was to compensate for inferiority at sea, for which purpose 220 bombers, over one hundred fighter and reconnaissance planes and four to five

1 Cf. Hubatsch, pp. 48–49.

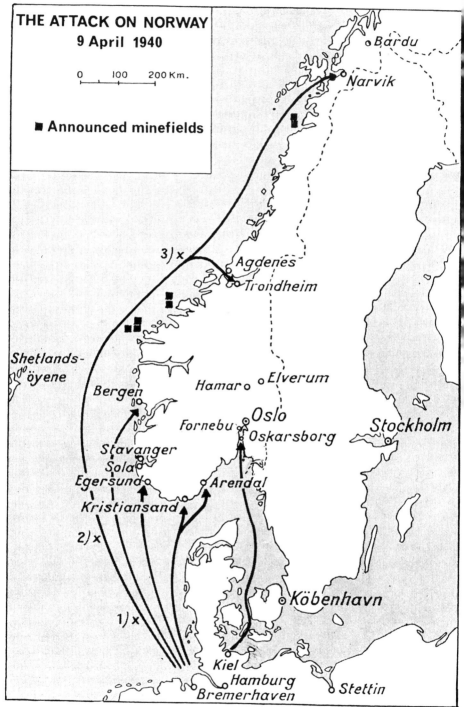

THE ATTACK ON NORWAY
9 April 1940

0   100   200 Km.

■ **Announced minefields**

Bardu

Narvik

Shetlands-
öyene

Agdenes

Trondheim

Bergen

Hamar

Elverum

Oslo

Fornebu

Oskarsborg

Stockholm

Stavanger

Sola

Egersund

Kristiansand

Arendal

3) x

2) x

1) x

Köbenhavn

Kiel

Hamburg

Bremerhaven

Stettin

1) and 2) Contact with British planes 3) Contact with British warships

hundred transport planes were actually ready for action in Scandinavia when the invasion was eventually carried out.[1]

As it seemed in those early days of March 1940, the operational orders were prepared not a moment too soon. Tension was now steadily mounting over Scandinavia, as it became increasingly evident that Finnish resistance was weakening. On 6 March General Halder noted in his diary: "England and France have demanded right of passage through Norway and Sweden. The Führer will act. On 10th preparations finished. 15th start *Weserübung*. Believes possible start of greater enterprise in west three days later." On the following day Hitler confirmed the final and last-minute alterations to the plans.

On 10 March, however, the picture began to change, as the news of the negotiations between Finland and the Soviet Union reached Berlin. As Jodl noted at the time, although the news might be politically satisfactory, the prospects were disturbing from a military viewpoint, since the conclusion of an armistice in Finland would make it difficult to motivate Falkenhorst's operation. Then, as Jodl on 12 March noted that everything except the ice conditions in the Baltic approaches allowed for 20 March as "*Weser* Day", he also added: "The peace Finland-Russia deprives England, but us as well, of the political basis for action in Norway."

The armistice between Finland and the Soviet Union was arranged just before midnight on 12 March. The resulting mood among the military leaders in three different countries, who had planned action in Norway under cover of the Finnish war, was perhaps understandably one of widespread disappointment lest all the work might have been in vain. Such fears, as previously shown, proved well-founded in Great Britain and to a large extent also in France. But in Germany, where the preparations were more advanced in size and thoroughness if not in timing, there proved also to be greater reluctance to wipe the plans off the board. On both 13 and 14 March, Jodl's diary records that Hitler was searching for new reasons or justifications that would allow *Weserübung* to take its course. Even Raeder was now expressing doubts

1 Hubatsch, p. 408.

as to the necessity of preventive action in Norway, and the suggestion was put forward of reversing the timetable and letting "Yellow" or the western offensive come before *Weserübung*. But that would create the danger that the violation of Belgian and Dutch neutrality would offer the Allies a good pretext for seizing Narvik.

Meanwhile, *Weserübung* remained on the agenda. Any sign that an Anglo-French action in Norway was still in preparation was investigated by the Naval Staff, and on 26 March a lengthy entry in the naval war diary was devoted to this question.[1] It countains a compilation of the unmistakable evidence that an action had been in the making at the time of the armistice in Finland, but goes on to state that "the question whether [the danger of] a British landing in Norway is still acute at present, must in my [Raeder's] opinion be negatived". On the other hand, the Naval War Command considered that the British in the time to come would most probably continue their attemps at hindering German traffic in neutral waters, and seek to provoke incidents that might possibly provide an excuse for action against Norway. This led them to the following and, as it seems, final conclusion: "Sooner or later Germany will have to face the question of carrying out *Weserübung*. The execution should therefore come as soon as possible—at least before 15 April, as thereafter the nights will be too short. There is a new moon on 7 April." Further support for this conclusion was found in the existing high level of preparedness, which could not be continued for very long without paralysing the whole of the German navy.

The time had come. *Weserübung* had acquired a life of its own and its own momentum; and there was no longer the question of a pretext, but of an opportunity. In three weeks the Germans had turned a full circle from the desire to exploit the threat of British action in Norway to Raeder's present determination that "Britain must not be given any pretext now for action against Norway".

1 Hubatsch, pp. 365—66.

44

9 April 1940. The German cruiser "Blücher" destroyed by the guns and torpedoes of Oscarsborg fortress in the Oslo fjord.

THE ONSLAUGHT

On 2 April Hitler held a top-level military conference in Berlin on the impending operations in Scandinavia, attended by *Generaloberst* Keitel as head of the OKW, *Generalfeldmarschall* Göring as head of the air force and *Grossadmiral* Raeder as head of the navy. Also present were General von Falkenhorst, the appointed leader of *Weserübung*, and his chief of staff Buschenhagen. At this meeting Falkenhorst confirmed that the weather and ice conditions in the relevant areas were now favourable to the air and naval operations foreseen for the invasion.[1] Hitler thereupon ordered the occupation of Denmark and Norway to take place on 9 April, with 0515 German time (0415 Norwegian time) as *"Weser* Hour".

Although the final decision had thus been taken, and the

1 Hubatsch, pp. 58 and 367.

45

first transport ships for the most distant invasion targets in Norway accordingly sailed from German harbours a few hours later, there still remained some points in the operational plans where further information would be useful. For this purpose, and on Hitler's orders, Colonel Piekenbrock of the German intelligence service had a pre-arranged meeting with Vidkun Quisling at the Hotel d'Angleterre in Copenhagen on 3 April to gather information about Norwegian defences.[1] According to Piekenbrock, although the information given was not sufficiently precise to be of decisive value, Quisling readily told him what he knew.

Whatever Quisling may have expected in return for his information, Piekenbrock was not empowered to reveal to him anything about the German plans that were now being translated into action. It must remain a moot point how much a trained staff officer like Quisling could deduce from this and previous conversations with his German contacts, as well as what he could see of the ice conditions in the Baltic approaches on his way to and from Copenhagen.

Secrecy and surprise were paramount to the success of *Weserübung*. The movement and assembly of ships and men at the end of March and beginning of April nevertheless gave rise to rumours in neutral and enemy circles that something was in the making. Guesses about the destination of the ships ranged over a wide area, but on 5 April the first indication reached the authorities in Oslo that Norway might be the target[2]. However, the vagueness of this warning gave it small odds against the fundamental improbability of such an eventuality, and at any rate its significance was soon lost under the impact of more manifest signs that something was being prepared against Norway in London and Paris. The notes to Norway from the British and French Governments that evening, previously referred to, clearly portended some unspecified later action in Norwegian waters.[3] At least in the eyes of Koht, the Norwegian

---

[1] Cf. IMT, Vol. 28, p. 418, Doc. 1809—PS, and articles by S. Hartmann in *Samtiden* 1956 No. 5 p. 317 seq. and in *Dagbladet* of 30 April 1965.

[2] *UK Report*, p. 86.

[3] Text of the note in *UK Report, Appendices*, Vol. II, pp. 242—43.

A German plane preparing to land at Oslo airport on 9 April. (Right:) The Norwegian soldiers had hardly any anti-aircraft weapons.

Foreign Minister, efforts to stop whatever action the Allies had planned now took precedence, since he believed that Germany would only act against Norway on direct enemy provocation.

However, before Koht's diplomatic efforts had materialised in a note of protest, the Allies proceeded to the next point on their timetable. In the early hours of 8 April the British navy laid a minefield in the approaches to Narvik, followed by the delivery of a note in Oslo announcing the action.[1] What the note did not reveal was that the two brigades of the 49th (Territorial) Division and one battalion of the 24th (Guards) Brigade were embarked on ships in Scotland, ready to meet possible German reactions to the minelaying.

But this was no longer of any importance; in fact the expedition was rapidly becoming a thing of the past, overtaken by greater events. Already on the previous evening the Admiralty had issued orders to the cruisers to disembark the troops and prepare for a major naval emergency, following reports of large-scale German movements in the North Sea[2]. The orders reached the 1st Cruiser Squadron late in the morning of 8 April, and by 2 p.m. the ships were ready to leave Rosyth naval base.

In Norway, the French and British notes on the mine-laying appear to have overshadowed everything else that day. Just after

1 *Ibid*, pp. 244—47.
2 Roskill, pp. 161—62.

German troops entering Akershus Castle in Oslo on 9 April.

mid-day Foreign Minister Koht informed the press of the contents of a sharp note of protest which he had drafted, and the rest of the afternoon was occupied by debates in the Storting and the Cabinet on the new situation caused by the mine-laying. The immediate urgency of staving off this new threat, before a vicious circle of actions and reactions could begin to form, appears to have blinded both the Foreign Minister and others concerned to the threat from another direction: for that same afternoon, information to the—as it now seems, inevitable—effect that a German invasion was on its way came in a telegram from London which said that German naval forces had been observed in the North Sea and might be arriving at Narvik before midnight. A short time afterwards it was also reported that German soldiers saved from a torpedoed steamer off southern Norway had said they were on their way to Bergen to protect Norway against the British.

Actually, increasingly reliable reports of a major breakout of the German navy had reached London already on 6 and 7 April. But the Admiralty, apparently exclusively worried about possible threats to their Atlantic supply lines, allowed their ships at sea to proceed on a course which in effect prevented all but chance encounters with the German invasion fleet.

A German destroyer sunk by the British Navy near Narvik four days after the invasion.

At any rate, the surprise effect of the German assault was achieved, and the opening shots of the Norwegian campaign in the night of 8–9 April caught the Norwegians both mentally and physically unprepared. Even after the news that foreign warships were entering the territory had reached a hastily assembled Cabinet soon after midnight, the Ministers, steeped in the niceties of peace-time politics and diplomacy, failed to issue a clearcut order for immediate and general mobilisation. Hence, at most of the landing points, the armed resistance to the German assault was improvised and inadequate, and did little more than delay the invasion timetable. Nevertheless the Government refused to accept Germany's ultimatum to surrender, and the resistance against the invaders in Oslofjord, where the German heavy cruiser *Blücher* was sunk with the spearhead of Germany's bold thrust to paralyse the national Government, gave the King and the Government the respite needed to escape to Hamar in central Norway. Here, and later in a neighbouring village

The German advance through Norway was aided by the early arrival of tanks.

further east, behind an improvised road-block which in the night defeated a second attempt to nip the armed Norwegian resistance in the bud, a hurried stock-taking could begin. And the result, announced through the King's rejection of the German proposal that the Government should give way to a Quisling ministry, was that Norway would fight on despite the grim outlook which the military situation presented.

The Campaign

General Otto Ruge, who now took over as Commander-in-Chief, formed his plans for a fighting retreat of his scattered forces on the assumption that the promptly promised assistance from the Allies would materialize before German superiority had crushed organized Norwegian resistance. On 14 April, as the German forces began their fan-shaped advance from the Oslo area into the surrounding countryside, the King addressed an urgent appeal to all Norwegians that "each individual do whatever he can to save the freedom and independence of our beloved country". On the

Norwegian ski troops in the Narvik area.

same day, advance parties of British troops were landed on the coast, north of Trondheim and in northern Norway. On the following day, the Army High Command issued a directive to the Norwegian forces which stated that Allied assistance was on the way. "Under these circumstances our task in the eastern part of the country is to gain time and keep up the struggle until assistance arrives, so as to be able to cooperate with the Allied forces." On the assumption that strong Allied assistance would be forthcoming, this seemed the only sensible strategy. Moreover, in several places the defenders were able to use their knowledge of the terrain and natural conditions to force the German attackers to halt their advance, at least temporarily. But already, after less than a week of steady retreat, some of the Norwegian forces were becoming demoralized, and some units were surrendering or crossing the border into Sweden.

On the tenth day of the campaign, the first British forces reached the front in central Norway. This should have been the signal for a change of strategy. But the troops were British territorials, inadequately trained and ill-equipped for warfare in winter conditions. A crucial point in the struggle for south/central Norway was reached on 22/23 April, when the Germans broke

51

through the Norwegian and British defences at the entrance to the main north-south valleys. Even worse, the strategy on which the British operations in Southern Norway had been based was already falling to pieces. Trondheim was the key to any attempt to regain control of Southern Norway. The original British plan had been to recapture central Norway with Trondheim and its important airfield by means of two pincer movements, one from the north and one from the south. But inadequate forces, and total German superiority in the air, made it increasingly doubtful whether the operation had any chance of success. On 25 April, therefore, the British Joint Planning Staff began planning for the withdrawal from Southern Norway, and on the evening of 27 April the order was issued to British forces to begin their evacuation. General Ruge's protests were in vain, and his exhausted and partly demoralized forces could do little more than cover the British retreat. In isolated pockets, Norwegian forces still offered determined resistance. But it was now only a matter of time before Southern Norway would have to be abandoned to the German invaders.

In Northern Norway, the campaign had developed in a completely different way. With the assistance of regular British, French and Polish forces, and immensely encouraged by the British navy's successful elimination of the German naval force at Narvik – partly due to the fact that the British navy could here operate largely out of reach of the German air force – the Norwegian forces had (before the end of April) succeeded in stemming the German advance and had taken the offensive. As the Norwegian Government and the High Command moved to Tromsö after the evacuation of Southern Norway, there seemed a real possibility that the combined strength of the Allies would succeed in ejecting the Germans from the Narvik area. Unfortunately, valuable time was lost due to the postponement, for various reasons, of the final assault on the German forces in the area. In the meantime, the Germans tried desperately to supply their forces in the area from the air. At the same time, a German regiment was making rapid progress in the seemingly impossible task of moving overland from the Trondheim area northwards in the direction of Narvik. The distance was enormous, natural obstacles were plentiful, and both Norwegian and British forces stood in their way.

On 13 May, the assault on the German forces in the surroundings of Narvik began. The final battle of Narvik was approaching. But time was getting short, and soon it would be too late. On 23 May, the lightning German offensive against Belgium and France which had begun on 10 May forced Churchill's War Cabinet to reconsider the whole war situation. And two days later, the British commander of the Allied forces in Northern Norway received the order to evacuate his forces as soon as possible, first conquering Narvik, if possible, in order to destroy the facilities for ore export to Germany and to cover the Allied withdrawal from Norway. And on 28 May, just as preparations were begun to abandon Bodö further south, French and Norwegian forces, heavily supported by units of the British navy, stormed the Narvik peninsula. By 5 p.m. the city was in Norwegian hands, and the German forces were retreating in the direction of the Swedish border. But on 1 June, as German troops entered Bodö, the British Government informed the Norwegian Foreign Minister of the decision to evacuate all Allied forces from Norway. After some hesitation, during which an attempt was made to explore a Swedish suggestion for the neutralization of Northern Norway, the Norwegian Government on 7 June made its final decision to abandon the struggle for Norway and move into exile in Britain. That same evening, the King and Crown Prince, together with most of the ministers, sailed from Tromsö aboard a British cruiser bound for Britain. And on 9 June, General Ruge, who had chosen to remain and face war imprisonment with his troops, contacted the German High Command with a request for an armistice. That evening, the King and Government proclaimed to the Norwegian people that their decision to leave the country did not mean the abandonment of the struggle to regain Norwegian independence. The struggle would be carried on outside the country's borders. On the following day, 10 June, General Ruge's representatives signed the agreements providing for the capitulation of the remaining Norwegian forces in Northern Norway.

AFTERTHOUGHTS

A defeat such as that inflicted on Norway in 1940 is inevitably followed by the popular game of "finding the guilty ones". Historians are not very good at this game; the "judgement of history", whatever it means, is seldom the judgement of historians. The brief, unequivocal and damning conclusions as to what did happen, should or might have happened, are usually alien to a conscientious search for the nearest approximation to objective historical truth.

However, the historian must also at times be willing to use the surgeon's knife, to cut away the malignant growth of legend and distortion that tends to develop on painful sections of the past. Regarding Norwegian neutrality up to 9 April 1940, the frequent but extravagant accusations about the Government's criminal or stupid handling of the situations that arose are emotional, not historical, judgements. However weak, ineffective, short-sighted or clumsy that Government's actions may at times have been, it should also be recognised that they were inspired by an honest and burning desire to remain at peace with other nations, and they were supported by an overwhelming majority of the Norwegian people. Moreover, there was nothing in their policy which entitled other powers to a massive violation of Norwegian territory under pretext of international law. As to the lack of foresight, of which the Government stands condemned by the events, it should be remembered that it was the whole nation which was caught mentally and physically unprepared. Nor, for that matter, was the lack of foresight limited to Norway.

Considering the Norwegian *Kriegsschuldfrage* as between Germany and the Western Allies, the current but naively schematic time-table comparisons of plans and preparations on both sides, propped up by suitable quotations from Churchill's pregnant prose, cannot explain away the fact that the actions actually undertaken by each of the opposing camps were different both in scope and in character. The comparatively minor British violations of Norwegian territory in the *Altmark* affair and the mine-laying on 8 April, flagrant though they were, could neither by law nor by equity justify the full-scale assault carried out by the

The King and the Crown Prince during a pause in the German bombing of the town of Molde.

Germans—even before the second of these violations was known to them. The irrelevant phrase about Germany "forestalling an Anglo-French action against Norway" may have a vaguely retaliatory and even defensive ring to many ears, but the fact remains that not even the rudimentary and somewhat Machiavellian standards of international law can provide any justification for Germany's invasion of Norway in 1940. As long as a spade is a spade, the invasion will stand as a plainly aggressive exercise in power politics.

Norway under occupation

GERMAN POLICY: CO-OPERATION WITH THE NORWEGIANS

Norway's decision to resist the German aggression confronted the invaders with a situation for which they seem to have been almost totally unprepared. *Weserübung* had been planned with the customary thoroughness of German staff work on the military side. Possible complications had been studied as far as they lent themselves to analysis, and alternative solutions had been embodied in orders and instructions. The whole operation still remained a gamble, but by no means a foolhardy one. In fact it had developed from what seemed to be rather a preposterous idea into something entirely feasible, if the German luck held --and it did, except on the political side.

German political views on the future relationship between occupied Norway and the Third Reich were based, as far as they went, on the assumption that the weight of events, and the presence of Germans in the most important ports, would make the Norwegian Government bow to the inevitable and seek a working arrangement with the occupying power. The German conditions for such an arrangement were summed up in the memorandum presented to Dr. Koht by Minister Bräuer in the early hours of 9 April. Severe as they might seem, they represented only a first stage. A second and more comprehensive set of obligations to be undertaken by Norway had been forwarded to Bräuer, to be presented at a later date when binding arrangements had been made. Thus, Norway was to have been led into a state of affairs which gave Germany umhampered control over almost anything that might be described as a valuable asset to German warfare.[1]

But Dr. Bräuer had received no instructions telling him what to do if the Norwegian Government refused to co-operate; nor

[1] For a full treatment of the period April—September 1940, see Skodvin, *Striden om okkupasjonsstyret* (Oslo, 1956).

The village of Elverum, bombed after the King there rejected Bräuer's second attempt to stop the armed resistance against the invaders.

had the military leaders of the *Weserübung,* apart from the order to crush possible resistance efficiently and ruthlessly. No policy had been provided with the possibility in mind that the Germans might find themselves without a Norwegian Government to deal with. This turned out to be the weak spot in the German plans, and it gave Norwegian resistance a much needed breathing-space and an initial advantage.

The task of organizing the new form of political co-operation with the Norwegians fell to Dr. Bräuer, who according to his instructions was the sole representative of the German Reich on Norwegian territory. In the absence of new directives from Berlin, he did what any trained diplomat could be expected to do: he tried to continue the same policy under different and admittedly more adverse circumstances. At noon on 9 April he approached the Ministry of Foreign Affairs, where a skeleton staff had remained on duty after the evacuation in the early morning. His purpose was to renew contact with the Norwegian Government in the hope that on second consideration they might still accept the terms of the memorandum. His messages were passed on, and on the following day Minister Bräuer was received by the King "somewhere in Norway"—at Elverum.

But in the meantime the political scene had changed rapidly and perhaps decisively. Quisling had entered upon the scene. At 7.32 p.m. on 9 April he managed to broadcast a speech over the Oslo radio transmitter in which he proclaimed a new government with himself as prime minister. The Nygaardsvold cabinet, he said, had been deposed and all "good Norwegians" were admonished to co-operate with himself and his new régime.

Quisling's proclamation no doubt clarified the situation considerably. To most Norwegian listeners it seemed obvious that this was the real German plan. Quisling was to be Hitler's man in Oslo. It may well be, in fact it would seem natural, that Quisling had been designated to play a role in the future "new order" in Norway. There is however no evidence that he had any secret understanding with Hitler as to his take-over bid on 9 April, apart from a few vague allegations from the Rosenberg camp and some rather tenuous deductions from military documents.

The idea of a Quisling coup in Norway had been dismissed by the German planners at an early stage as entirely unrealistic. About the practical side of *Weserübung* Quisling knew as little as anybody else. But he knew perfectly well how seriously Hitler considered an invasion of Norway, and was prepared to assist in his way. So on 8 April he drew his own conclusions and decided to take the plunge. And this could mean but one thing. Quisling was not a man of political subtleties, and to play a role in politics to him meant to take over power. He believed it possible to leap right to the top of the pyramid. So he sat down at his desk in the Hotel Continental and wrote his proclamation, including a list of cabinet members, most of whom he had been unable to consult. Among those who were outside Oslo, even old party members reacted with hesitation and reluctance, while others flatly expressed their surprise and indignation; two who were regular officers reported instead for duty with their army units.

Quisling's way to the broadcasting studio in Oslo had been opened by a cabal of the kind that seems to thrive in such apparently monolithic structures as the Third Reich. He was encouraged and assisted by Rosenberg's man Scheidt and by *Grossadmiral* Raeder's representative, Captain Schreiber. Minister Bräuer had no instructions to co-operate with Quisling, did not approve of Quisling's initiative, and in fact was taken entirely by surprise. He called Berlin for guidance and was finally able to reach Foreign Minister Ribbentrop. Ribbentrop, however, did not want to commit himself, and after another delay Hitler himself came to the telephone. He instructed Bräuer, in no uncertain terms, to support Quisling.

Bräuer interpreted this to mean that there was to be no compromise on the demand for Quisling as prime minister, whereas the composition of his cabinet remained a matter for negotiation. To Bräuer this was a very serious handicap, but he was unable to impress his objections on Berlin. Without much hope he left for Elverum.

The King and Government had not refused renewed contact with the Germans, but only for the purpose of exploring possibilities, and on certain conditions such as the cessation of hostilities during possible negotiations. Warning voices had not failed to point out that, regardless of German assurances to the contrary, a new régime was likely to be established soon in Oslo. The Quisling incident confirmed the worst suspicions, and the King thereupon declared his unwillingness and inability to accept a prime minister whom the people would not approve and would in fact reject.

THE CONSISTENCY OF GERMAN POLICY

From now on, two German policies compete in Norway. Dr. Bräuer, an able diplomat with a good understanding of political life in Norway, envisages a régime willing to acceut a certain measure of collaboration with Germany, and able to do so without losing the necessary minimum of political support in the country. This immediately makes Quisling unacceptable to him. Hitler, on the other hand, enraged at the stubbornness and stupidity of this ridiculously small country and its petty king, insists on a drastic change. The Norwegians had refused his outstretched hand; now his will was to be forced upon them.

Bräuer, weighing his own judgement against Hitler's decision, tried with considerable talent to reconcile these openly conflicting policies. The result was the appointment on 15 April of *Administrasjonsrådet* (the Administrative Council), a name which implies executive powers only and excludes policy-making. The Administrative Council was an emergency comittee to deal with such practical problems as came up in the occupied territory outside the reach of the central Government. It arose from the Norwegian desire for some kind of central authority, and was approved by the members of the Supreme Court, the only constitutional authority that remained in the capital. For political reasons of his own, Bräuer also approved it.

In favourable conditions, above all the successful progress of Germany's war in Norway, the Administrative Council in Bräuer's opinion might have gone a long way towards providing an alternative political solution.[1] It replaced the Quisling "government" which he regarded as a futile venture. For a brief moment the Council even seemed acceptable to the King, although this hope had to be discarded. Bräuer further thought it might provide the nucleus of a future new government acceptable to the people; it might, if the worst came to the worst, grow into a rival government. In all events the Administrative Council seemed to be as close as Bräuer could get to the original plan and to his own policy. His policy failed, but it was skilfully conceived, with a measure of understanding of the political possibilities in Norway which Hitler failed to grasp.

The Führer wanted a clear-cut decision in Norway, and would have no qualms about imposing it. Bräuer therefore pursued his own policy at severe risk, including a certain amount of duplicity. He thus led Hitler to belive that a new, collaborationist government was being organized, while allowing the Norwegian negotiators to insist on the apolitical nature of the new council. When this contradiction became known to Hitler, at a time of mounting crisis over Narvik, his indignation turned towards Bräuer, who was barely able to resign before the storm broke. It was the end of Bräuer's diplomatic career, and his special adviser sent up from Germany suffered the same

1 On the Administrative Council, see *UK Report*, Part II.

Reichskommissar Terboven speaks. (Right:) "Ministerpresident" Vidkun Quisling reviewing troops in front of the Royal Palace in Oslo.

fate. He was Theodor Habicht, of Austrian fame and therefore presumably regarded as a specialist on misguided Germanic peoples.

The Administrative Council, however, was by then a fact and continued to exist until 25 September 1940. Its duties were distributed among the members in accordance with the normal division of labour between Norwegian governmental departments, and the Council's functions generally remained at a nonpolitical level. This was possible partly because of the expressed determination to that effect on the part of the Council members, and partly because throughout this period Germany was experimenting with new forms of occupation government in Norway; this led into many unexplored avenues of occupation policy, and probably set precedents or provided experiences that affected the solution of similar problems in other occupied territories, notably in the Netherlands.

Hitler was under considerable strain in the days following Bräuer's fall. He came very near to giving up the German position at Narvik, and was surrounded by both political and military tensions. The situation had all the makings of a crisis of the first order. In the problem of the Norwegian occupation government, Hitler fell back upon the familiar device of appointing an old party-fighter as his special trouble-shooter. In this way, Joseph Terboven came to Norway as Reich Commissioner.

The title of *Reichskommissar* had repeatedly been used, long before Hitler's time, to provide special authority for representatives of the central German government commissioned to deal with emergency situations for which the normal civil service was not prepared or adequately equipped. To this traditional scope of the *Reichskommissar* Hitler had added the function of a political or party *Reichskommissar*, resulting in a particularly strong concentration of power in the hands of trusted men. In great haste, the Gauleiter in Essen and President of the Rhine Province, Terboven, was now summoned to Berlin and ordered to proceed to Norway with such staff as he was able to assemble at short notice. He took over officially on 24 April 1940, and the *Reichskommissariat für die besetzten Gebiete Norwegens* was to function throughout the war.

Terboven came to Norway with two principal policy aims: first, to use his new authority to further Germany's efforts to win the war, and second, to organize an occupation government that would be able to function. The second task was of course subordinate to the first.

There is a highly interesting comparison to be made between Dr. Bräuer, German Minister to Oslo and later *Reichsbevollmächtigter* (Reich plenipotentiary) for about a week, and Terboven who remained *Reichskommissar* in occupied Norway until he was dismissed a few days before the German surrender. Though strikingly different from most points of view, they remained similar in their attempts to find somebody to work with in Norway, somebody with a political strength and backing of his own who did not have to borrow his authority from the invaders and sit on their bayonets. They did not expect any useful partnership from a marionette government in Norway, and in this they revealed a real understanding of the significance of power in a situation of this kind.

They did, however, seek potential partners in very different quarters. Bräuer had turned to elements within the old system because he had seen how deeply rooted it was in Norwegian life. He had himself experienced parliamentary democracy in Germany without coming to despise it, and as a diplomat he had been trained to understand its processes and within limits to respect it, at least to the extent that its continued existence could be reconciled with his own loyalty to the state he had chosen to serve. For such reasons he had tried to organise some kind of *modus vivendi* with the legal Norwegian Government, or some similar arrangement.

Terboven was very different, both as a man and in terms of his political background and experience. Bred as a political fist-fighter in the streets of one of the "red" strongholds of the Weimar Republic, he had risen to power with Hitler and in 1940 found himself at the top of the party hierarchy as one of the leading *Gauleiters*. He could rise no higher, unless he penetrated into the rather closed circle around Hitler.

The political system which the Norwegians had devised for themselves meant nothing to Terboven, except as a means to an end. But he did realize to what extent Norwegians rallied behind it, especially in this time of crisis, so he decided to use it as a tool. Through a semblance of continuity, Norway was to be led into increasing degrees of collaboration with Hitler's Germany, partly falling, partly being pushed, and possibly without being too much aware of the changes. The Norwegians, it was thought, would hardly regroup their forces and make a determined stand as long as the political scenery seemed familiar. The sheer weight of the German presence in the country, including his own, would wear down resistance. Terboven was determined to carry out this policy ruthlessly, only stopping short of the breaking point. He tried to do it during the summer of 1940 but failed, and had to improvise a substitute solution on 25 September.

All the elements that were later to dominate political developments in occupied Norway appeared in the summer months of 1940: general collaborationism, Norwegian versions of national-socialism, the organisation of German political control and the foundations of resistance. In this interplay of political forces, Vidkun Quisling played a rather hesitant and self-conscious role in political semi-obscurity, from which he emerged during August 1940 to assume a role of leadership for which he was neither endowed nor equipped. With the organisation of the "Council of Commissioner Ministers" in September 1940, the political situation froze as far as the distribution of power was concerned. The German *Reichskommissariat* assumed full control, leaving to the NS or *Nasjonal Samling* such functions as seemed expedient. Formal changes of status were to follow: "Commissioner Ministers" became "Ministers" a year later, and a "national government" was formed on 1 February 1942, in which Quisling himself for the first time assumed office as "*Ministerpresident*". But no real re-distribution of power occurred, nor was it seriously contemplated in Germany, except perhaps for a brief period in the second half of 1941.

RESISTANCE AND COLLABORATION

The main theme of Norwegian history 1940–45 is without doubt the resistance movement, as organised and carried out by the Government abroad and by "Home Front" leaders in Norway. Its origins, its growth, its organisation, its widening scope, its multiple activities, its tests of strength, its defeats, its final triumph that gave Norway a small but undisputed, and to Norwegians significant, place among the victorious Allies—this is what Norwegian history during the Second World War is about. But the history of resistance in Norway can here only be outlined in the general context as a contrasting background to the main object of this study—the record of collaborationism in Norway and the role and importance of Quisling and his party.

In general terms, the summer of 1940 has been characterised diversely as a period of defeatism, of suspense and of clarification. It may well be described as a combination of the three, a period of stumbling along between hope, hesitation and apathy, as the will to resist, manifest from the very day of the German landing, groped to define its aims more precisely, to determine a line of action and to gather strength. At the end of the campaign which lasted for two months, the long and slow process of building a new and clandestine military force began. Political resistance centred around energetic pressure groups, which took immediate action to prevent that quasi-legal settlement with the occupying power which was embedded in Terboven's plan for a new government to be legalized by the Stor-

With no petrol available under the occupation, cars ran on gas generated by wood or carbide burners mounted on the back.

ting—the so-called *Riksråd* or Council of the Realm. Terboven wanted the Storting to appoint such a council and then fade away, thus leaving the *Riksråd* alone on the political stage with full powers to act both as legislator and as an executive and policy-making body. The *Riksråd* was to be composed of men who, taken together, possessed the required amount of public confidence, but also had the required minimum of susceptibility to German pressure. Through this back door, full collaborationism was gradually to infiltrate, if Terboven had his way.

There was no room for Quisling in Terboven's plan. The *Reichskommissar* had immediately sized him up as a vague and inefficient theoretician, and the Third Reich was to offer him no political career in Norway. He was not such stuff as Führers are made of. To give him an honourable retreat, however, Terboven decided to send him away, preferably to Germany so that he would not again get in the way. He was to be offered some glorified state of political insignificance such as, for instance, the study of history, pensioned off from practical politics where he did not belong. In fact, Quisling was sent to Germany early in July 1940; but soon after his arrival in Berlin, he escaped from his deporters and was again taken under the wing of his protector Rosenberg. With the latter's assistance, as well as that of *Grossadmiral* Raeder, he was able to make his partial come-back in Norwegian politics in September 1940.

These events provide the background to the history as well as the legend of Quisling's struggle against Terboven and, some would say, against the Germans. It is both a matter of history and of legend inasmuch as it is, undoubtedly, based on fact and, equally undoubtedly, magnified into a glorious "patriot-Quisling" image which has no foundation whatsoever in reality. The notorious differences and frictions between Quisling and Terboven fall into the category of internal bickerings that seem to arise automatically among partners. As far as the nazi *Gleichschaltung* of Norway was concerned the two of them differed to a certain extent about ways and means, but they both wanted it and fought for it, hoping to see a national-socialist Norway as a result of the German victory to which their efforts were dedicated.

NS CONTROLLED BY REICHSKOMMISSAR

Terboven did not fight against or disapprove of the Norwegian sister party; he only found it absurdly small and inefficient. *Nasjonal Samling* was clearly unfit for a real political role until it could grow considerably in terms of membership and adherence and build up a party organisation. On the day of the German invasion such an organisation hardly existed. Membership dues had not been collected since 1936/37, and only a handful of sympathizers were still politically active in a few towns. Not even in Oslo had there been any regular party activity in 1938/39. Hence, Terboven had no confidence in the party's ability to develop, unless it was guided by a strong and not necessarily gentle German hand. He made it clear to NS leaders that they had to concentrate on recruiting members and learning practical party work, and brought advisers from Germany to control and direct NS party activities at all levels. The old guard of the NS of course resented this, but were unable to devise any constructive policy of their own.

At the same time Terboven toyed with the idea of stimulating the formation of a new party, mainly recruited from potential "Petain characters" in Norway, many of whom might be described as not opposed to the "New Germany" but definitely antagonized by Quisling. The *Reichskommissar* had considerable hope for the future of such a party, and not without reason. But he failed because those members of the Storting who were assembled in Oslo in August and September 1940 in the end refused to lend their support to the *Riksråd*. Thus Terboven's first requisite for a quasi-legal solution did not materialize. Moreover, Hitler himself finally interfered with Terboven's policy and decided early in August that, whatever new arrangements were to be made in Norway, Quisling should have a place in them. This meant that Terboven was unable to offer Quisling's disappearance as a prize for Norwegian political co-operation. However, the resilient *Reichskommissar* soon found a next-best solution—the "Commissioner Ministers"; Quisling himself was not included and the important fields of finance, trade and supplies were given to non-NS members.

Quisling himself always maintained that he was given a free choice by Hitler as regards his return to the scene in Norway. He could, as he put it, "take over" immediately, or he could wait for a while so as to appear with greater strength and be spared the onus of many unpopular measures which no doubt would have to be taken very soon. It had been clear from the beginning of August that German troops would remain in Norway through the winter, and the consequent burden on Norway's finances would coincide with a general decline in the standard of living. Quisling firmly believed that his accession to power had been promised to him after a period not exceeding six months, and such a time limit had indeed been mentioned between Terboven and Quisling. But there seems little doubt that, in Terboven's mind, this was to be a testing period and nothing more. The *Nasjonal Samling* could only be given a greater share in occupation government if and when the party proved able to plan and carry out constructive policies with sufficient support from the population. In the meantime the *Reichskommissar* was to remain the source of power, and the "Council of Commisioner Ministers" could hold no authority unless derived from the occupying power. Its "laws", for instance, had to be submitted to the *Reichskommissar* for approval before promulgation. Attempts to by-pass this control in minor matters were repeatedly rebuffed.

THE STRENGTH OF RESISTANCE

In the period from September 1940 till mid-summer 1941, while the Norwegian Government in London organised its contribution to Allied warfare, the resistance in Norway went through a similar period of organisation and of forming a policy. As a general trend in public opinion, the spirit of resistance soon showed its strength. The reports of the German *Sicherheitsdienst* in Norway almost monotonously repeated twice a month that resistance continued to stiffen. Centres of political resistance, as already mentioned, had formed already during the summer of 1940, acting as pressure groups during the *Riksråd* negotiations, or distributing information withheld by German censorship. Through their efforts, vital guidance such as the text of the King's refusal to abdicate in July 1940 was rapidly disseminated throughout the country, and appears to have been reproduced in tens of thousands of copies. During the following winter, these nuclei of organised resistance joined forces and began to channel into political action a strong but inarticulate opinion against the occupying power and its helpers.

A sociologist might describe the rise of Norwegian resistance as a case study in "the organisation society" assuming political functions.[1] The constitutional powers had disappeared from the political scene in Norway: the King and his Cabinet were in London, the Storting had been dismissed by Terboven, and the judges of the Supreme Court had resigned when they were denied what they held to be their constitutional right to review

[1] For a thorough study of this aspect of Norwegian resistance, see Th. Chr. Wyller, *Nyordning og Motstand* (Oslo, 1958).

The King's emblem painted on walls was a widespread symbol of protest against the occupation régime.

the *Reichskommissar's* legislation. Political meetings were not allowed, free discussion was impossible, censorship was widespread and the press was under daily control and received directives from the *Reichskommissariat*. In sum, normal political life had been made impossible in Norway.

The first mass reaction to this state of affairs was a rather naive but natural urge to "do something". Sporadic fist-fights and street-riots occurred and demonstrations became the order of the day, particularly after the NS started a propaganda offensive in October and November: loud-speakers exploded, speakers were booed, and so forth. All these spontaneous reactions represented a body of opinion looking for a new organisational framework after the familiar political structure had been torn down. In this situation the existing pattern of social organisation took over. Voluntary movements, professional organisations, the whole network of formalized social groups, somehow associated with the break-through of political democracy in Norway, mobilized for political purposes in defence of what they felt was an integral part of their heritage.

The medical association, for instance, protested strongly against interference such as the appointment of NS members to positions for which they did not appear qualified. A very efficient contribution came from the civil servants, who reacted against the institution of an NS "civil service bureau" and its proclaimed policy of preference for party members for public offices. During the winter months, contacts were made and liaison established between local branches until, in May 1941, no less than 43 professional organisations representing about 750,000 members delivered a formal protest to the *Reichskommissar* against the policy of nazification. In reprisal, the *Reichskommissar* appointed *kommissars* for these and other organisations, besides arresting many of the protesting chairmen.

At this point Norwegian resistance went underground, but without changing its basic structure. A committe of co-ordination *(Koordinasjonskomiteen)* was constituted, its members representing such professional groups as teachers, farmers, trade unionists and the clergy. Both structurally and in terms of the persons involved, the continuity from "legal" to "illegal" resistance seems very clear, and the committee of co-ordination was later to become the executive of the "Home Front" leadership.

However, this period also witnessed a certain growth and expansion of the *Nasjonal Samling*. Following the events of September 1940, the party received a considerable number of new members. Old members seem to have been rather sceptical about a number of the new ones, seeing them as fellow travellers with economic and similar suspect motives. On the other hand, national-socialists in Norway as elsewhere proved capable of appealing to the kind of easily moved enthusiasm that filled their ranks. The earliest, fairly reliable, membership figure dates from 27 August 1940 and shows a strength of 4,202 members.[1] By the end of December 1940 membership had risen to 23,755, more than 7,000 having joined in the month of October.

[1] This and following figures from *Om Landssvikoppgjøret* (Oslo, 1963).

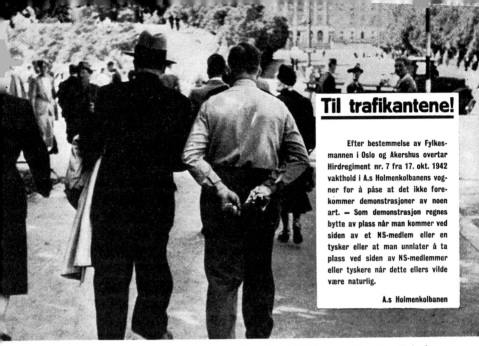

With his back to the photographer, one of Quisling's *Hird* men with a handful of flowers ripped off people who wore them to mark the King's birthday. The poster warns tram passengers against demonstrations such as refusing to sit beside NS people or Germans.

Party membership culminated in November 1943 with 43,400, and thereafter declined slightly through the rest of the war. All these figures refer to the NS party proper, excluding the youth organisation. In the following table, the first column shows membership of the youth organisation, and the second over-all membership, at intervals of four months during the period of significant growth:

Date			
1940	25.12	2,423	26,178
1941	1.4	3,601	29,428
	1.8	5,278	34,928
	1.12	5,894	39,306
1942	1.4	4,987	42,920

A closer examination of the enrolment figures reveals that the party was fairly insignificant in size as late as the beginning

of September 1940. The events of September, and the organisation of the "Council of Commissioner Ministers", led to a period of growth which lasted until the turn of the year. Through
1941, in spite of very energetic efforts, the trend was unsteady
with monthly variations ranging from over 1,000 new members
down to a net loss of a couple of hundreds. Until the mid-
summer of 1942 the party still received on average about 1,000
new members a month, from a total population of just over
three millions.

From mid-summer 1942 until the autumn of 1943 the party
continued to grow, however slightly, but in the twelve months
following November 1943 the party lost some 1,000 members,
and from then on the decline was never reversed. Statistics for
the last months, moreover, do not give a real picture of political opinion within the NS, since there seems to have been a
considerable amount of dissociation without actual cancellation of membership.

The NS was very much aware of the fact that its political
future depended on increasing membership, and the leaders of
the party paid great attention to enrolment figures. Whenever
Quisling pressed for an enlarged role for the party in Norwegian affairs, statistics were always used as a powerful argument. From a political point of view the act of joining the party
was therefore in itself a contribution towards strengthening
Quisling's aspirations.

A recruiting drive in the latter half of 1941 had as its immediate aim a numerical strength of 100,000 members, or 3.55 %
of Norway's total population. Each party district was given a
target figure in proportion to the resident population. None of
them made it. The best results up to April 1942 were reached
by the Oslo district, with 68,3 % of its quota, due no doubt to
the fact that so many party members were placed in party and
public administration in the capital. At the other end of the
scale, Sogn og Fjordane in the west stopped at 7 % of its allot-
ted number, and on average the district quotas were only filled
by one third.

Quisling himself still felt that the party was strong enough to
take over. In March 1941 he wrote to Dr. Lammers, the head of

Quisling greets soldiers of the Norwegian Legion on their return from the eastern front.

Hitler's Reich Chancellery, informing him that the NS now numbered 30,000, which in relation to population was "approximately the equivalent of the NSDAP's strength when it came to power".[1] Dr. Lammers did not bother to retort.

QUISLING'S MILITARY CO-OPERATION WITH GERMANY

The figures show that, although NS propaganda was given every encouragement and political opposition was heavily persecuted, the party never reached a size which enabled it to play a role independently of the Germans.

Nor was it able to rally its members around the idea of a "Norwegian national-socialism". Hence, as the war went on,

1 OPA (Oslo Police Archives), Quisling dossier.

and parallel with the ascendancy of Himmler in Germany, the substitute philosophy of the Greater Germanic idea gained currency.

This tendency was particularly noticeable among those who joined the SS, and therefore among those Norwegians who served with German units. Altogether about 5,000 Norwegian citizens did war service on the German fronts, and this recruitment of volunteers was another of the party's important functions. In comparison, the clandestine military resistance organisation mobilized more than 40,000 by the end of the war. In March 1945 about 2,000 Norwegians were on active German front service, and some 1,700 had been discharged. The NS year-book in 1942 listed 170 members killed in action and official post-war statistics have verified 689 deaths. Real losses must have been higher, perhaps in the neighbourhood of 1,000.

The idea of admitting Norwegians to German military service had been brought up in 1940 by Quisling in a letter to the Reich Chancellery requesting that Norwegians should be admitted to "voluntary war service in the German army". This was then granted, but only a few men volunteered. Later, a long series of special "Nordic" units was organised, although all of these were in practice dominated by the Germans.

The *Standarte Nordland* had been created by Himmler in May 1940, but its Norwegian birthday was 12 January 1941, when it was first proclaimed by Quisling himself over the radio. This occurred before the Soviet Union's entry into the war, and Quisling's appeal called for both solidarity with the Third Reich and participation in the war against Great Britain. He invited all young Norwegians to join the "general European war of freedom and independence against the English world-despotism—a fight that must end with the defeat of England . . . Germany", he said, "has not asked us to come. We ourselves feel duty-bound to march freely and firmly to the very end along the road which destiny has marked for our people. Norway and Germany have common interests. Germany's victory is Norway's victory!"[1]

The *Standarte Nordland* was intended to group Danish,

1 *Fritt Folk*, 13 January 1941.

Swedish and Norwegian volunteers under German officers, forming part of SS division *Wiking*. Himmler, who took a special interest in Germanic volunteers, came to Oslo to muster the first group of Norwegians on the anniversary of Hitler's *Machtübernahme*, 30 January 1941. The Standarte was officially described in Norway as a regiment, but it never became one and was dissolved in the autumn of 1943.

Many of the men, however, continued their service in new formations which were being organised all the time. One of them, and probably the most ambitious, was the Norwegian Legion, promoted under the slogan of the "fight against Bolshevism". At the outset the officers were Norwegian, but after six months the Germans took over, and the men had to swear allegiance to Hitler. Their uniform was that of the German SS, but had a Norwegian flag on the arm and the Norwegian lion on the collar. Altogether about 2,000 men served in the Legion, which suffered severe losses near Leningrad in January 1942 and was dissolved in May 1943. The majority of the 700 surviving legionaries volunteered again, this time for the so-called *SS-Panzer-Grenadier-Regiment Norge*. Officially, this was intended to be "absolutely Norwegian" and to muster 3,000 men, but only about 700 could be found and the regiment had to be filled with Hungarian and Roumanian volunteers. The leader was a German. An SS "Norge" battalion of skiers later served in Finland and northern Norway, but was brought back to the south towards the end of the war. Some of them served in razzias against resistance units. Another SS unit served in German camps for deported Serbians and other foreign prisoners.

As a purely military contribution these units did not carry much weight. In the hecatomb of the eastern front, Quisling's units tended to disappear in the maelstrom as far as military strength was concerned, but Quisling himself attached considerable political importance to them. First, the volunteers for German service were to testify to his reliability as a partner. Second, he intended to build an army of his own.

The existence of such an army was proclaimed in Quisling's "law" of 14 August 1943, which stated that certain military and paramilitary formations would from then on be considered as belonging to the "armed forces of the realm". These formations were Quisling's personal "Führer Guard" (the *Germanske SS Norge)*, founded in July 1942 and bound by loyalty oaths to both Hitler and Quisling, and the *Hird,* as the Norwegian equivalent of the German SA. In these "armed forces" Quisling also included the regular Norwegian police, and maintained that for this reason the policemen came under military law. Two days later a Norwegian police officer was sentenced to death for declining to assist in the arrest of a couple of young girls who had refused to follow the summons to compulsory labour service. His "crime" took place before the "law" of 14 August 1943 existed. Such death sentences as were later pronounced by the special court of the Quisling régime were based on this "law".

QUISLING'S ALLY—NORWAY'S ENEMY

In this attempt to create an army of his own, Quisling went further than many of his closest supporters were prepared to follow. Some of his "ministers" opposed the measure, and the law of August 1943 therefore led to a serious split in Quisling's "cabinet". The controversy was aggravated when Quisling simultaneously brought up the whole problem of the relationship between Germany and occupied Norway, in particular whether a state of war did or did not exist. This question, though very clear to most Norwegians, was rather controversial within the NS. In the preamble to the above-mentioned "law", Quisling now produced a categorical statement without even consulting his "cabinet", with the result that the "ministers" immediately challenged his authority to act in this Führer-like manner.

Quisling's "law" opened with the following general statement: "A state of war has existed and prevails in Norway because of the aggressive actions of the Soviet Union and its allies against Norwegian territory and Norwegian citizens. Thus these states have acted as, and must in the sense of the law be considered as, enemies of Norway, the great German Reich and its associates as states allied with Norway".[1]

1 OPA, Quisling dossier.

In a letter of 31 August 1943 to Quisling,[1] "Minister" Irgens stated that the *"Ministerpresident"* had exceeded his authority, as in matters of such political significance his advisers ought to be consulted. Irgens felt that Quisling could only speak as a "head of state" when "surrounded by his council and acting in co-operation with it"—a line of reasoning consistent with the Norwegian constitution and political tradition, but of course contrary to Quisling's version of the Führer principle.

Irgens also summed up his views on the NS-German relationship, and stated that Quisling's declaration to the effect that Norway was associated with Germany, and in a state of war with Germany's enemies, was different from the official German opinion. He quoted the *Führer-Erlass* of 24 April 1940 which clearly said that the Norwegian Government, through its proclamation, its behaviour and the acts of war that took place on its orders, had created a state of war between Norway and the German Reich. Hitler's decision, published in the form of an Executive Order in the official German law gazette, had never been withdrawn or altered, and provided the legal foundation for German prize courts dealing with captured Norwegian ships. Moreover, on the very day when Quisling's "law" was announced, by rounding up Norwegian officers and treating them as prisoners of war, the Germans had made it perfectly clear that "they still considered themselves as being at war with Norway. Norway's legal and formal relationship with Germany cannot be settled in the preamble to a law, but must be regulated by an agreement between the governments of both countries. The necessary precondition for the negotiation of such an agreement is however that Norway has a real Norwegian government recognized by Germany. This was the situation expected to materialize after 1 February 1942, but which is still in abeyance."

Irgens concluded that there was no alliance between Germany and Norway nor any state of war with the Allied powers. A Norwegian law could therefore pronounce nothing to the contrary. If the occupying power was of the opinion that Norwegians, for instance in the police force, had violated laws of

1 OPA, Irgens dossier.

war, it must be up to the Germans to institute proceedings against them.

According to his own statement during the post-war trial, Quisling seems to have felt at that particular time that the Germans wanted a sentence of death against the police officer in question. He therefore found it advisable to provide for it on his own authority, so the Germans would not be able to claim that "the Norwegian government could no longer maintain its position".[1] Riisnæs, who was then "Minister of Justice", had quoted a statement by Terboven to the effect that a government so lacking in authority that it had to depend on the occupying power for the maintenance of discipline in the police force had placed itself in an impossible situation.[2]

The controversy around the "law" of 14 August 1943 shows that even within Quisling's own "cabinet" the opinion was held that Norway continued to be at war with Germany. The deep split that occurred in the atumn of 1943, however, had a long history. Ever since 1940, Quisling had hoped for some kind of treaty with Germany which would give his régime a formal status independent of the occupying power. Unable to obtain this, he gradually reduced his aims, talking no more of a peace treaty but of a provisional peace or *Vorfriede* and attempting a kind of functional approach, such as the beginnings of a consular service in Germany. At every point his hopes were frustrated, but he persisted and for a brief period around the turn of the year 1941—42 he had high hopes of success. For reasons of his own, Terboven had worked out an arrangement that gave Quisling an official position in the occupation government as *Ministerpresident* and converted the "Council of Commissioner Ministers" into a "national government". But Terboven, who had no confidence whatsoever in Quisling as a politician and realized to what extent his very existence was a powerful stimulus to increasing resistance in Norway, made it perfectly clear that no real change was contemplated. In a telephone conversation with his legal adviser, Schiedermair, who had been sent to Berlin in this connection, he stressed that as long as no real change occurred

1 *Straffesak mot V. Quisling* (Oslo, 1946), pp. 23 and 130 seq.
2 OPA, Riisnæs dossier.

78

1 February 1942: Terboven and Quisling arrive for the ceremony marking the establishment of a "national government" with Quisling as *Ministerpresident*.

in terms of authority and political power, forms did not matter.[1] Thus Quisling remained dependent on the *Reichskommissariat* for all practical purposes, and had to take his full share of the blame for such critical developments as the showdown with the church and the schools in 1942.

In outline, 1942 was the year when civilian resistance was able to show its full strength and widespread support all over Norway. The organisation network had been built up, secret communications had been organized, and close contact was established with political and military authorities in London, as well as with Norwegian agencies in Stockholm. The stage was set for a test of strength, and this occurred when Quisling, apparently without support, launched a campaign to assume control over teaching in schools and to prevent the church from speaking out against the "new order". Teachers were ordered to join a new organisation controlled by party members, and the clergy were told to stay out of "politics". Both groups refused to co-operate, and the teachers' union of the "new order" became an empty shell, while the state church broke with the "state". Arrests and deportations followed on a large scale.

From this time onwards it seems to have been the general opinion in German quarters that Quisling had to be written

1 Note of 29 January 1942. OPA, Quisling dossier.

off as a political failure. Since to let him fall openly would have involved a loss of face, he was allowed to remain in a semblance of authority; but there could be no question of such a thing as a peace treaty or even of any step in that direction. Repeated attempts by Quisling to open discussions, or at least to establish some kind of contact concerning these matters, were rebuked with an increasing impatience which soon turned into curtness bordering on discourtesy. Thus *Reichsminister* Lammers wrote on 17 September 1942 to remind Quisling that Hitler had already explained why the problem of German-Norwegian relations would have to wait, due to the prevailing state of war. The Führer had now instructed him to supplement this statement and to inform Quisling that a settlement of this problem could only follow after the end of the war. "The Führer wishes that there shall be no kind of negotiations or discussions during the war concerning a final or preliminary peace between the Greater German Reich and Norway or concerning other measures that in any way define or anticipate Norway's relationship with the Reich after the end of the war."[1] Moreover, Quisling was henceforth to have no contact with the Reich government except through the *Reichskommissar*, who alone was responsible for the civilian sector in Norway as the Führer's representative.

A few days later the *Reichskommissar*, while addressing a meeting of NS party leaders, offered his comments. The idea that "Norway will become free and independent after this war", he said, was "taken from the old democratic jargon". With national-socialism as their foundation, the Germanic peoples would grow together into one single great and powerful empire. At this point, Norwegians should therefore put their trust in the "unique greatness of the Führer" knowing that he would give to a Norway "for which national-socialist and greater germanic thought has become supreme law, time and free will to grow gradually into the united greater German empire through a sound development . . ."[2].

Such was the lesson for the leaders of the *Nasjonal Samling*

[1] OPA, Quisling dossier.
[2] War Collection, Oslo University, Institute of History.

80

on German intentions in Norway, at the moment when Quisling proclaimed his alliance with Germany and his war with Hitler's enemies, and most of them maintained a stronger sense of realism than their chief.

Thus, another of Quisling's "ministers" wrote in September 1944: "The Nygaardsvold government announced before its departure from the country that we were at war with Germany, and maintains this point of view as an exiled government in London. One must acknowledge that the major part of the Norwegian people has the same opinion . . . Germany and its representatives have in part revealed a rather unclear attitude to this problem. One could be tempted to say that they have at any given moment adopted the viewpoint that served their interests . . ."[1]

Perhaps the best summing up was given in the candid remarks of Quisling's adviser on foreign policy, Finn Støren, in March 1945. "I have a feeling that the German authorities are deliberately making fools of you, Mr. *Ministerpresident,* and of the *Nasjonal Samling* . . . As you yourself have pointed out, Norway is *de jure* at war with Germany . . . in spite of all the support that Norway under your government has given to Germany. The *de jure* state of war has served and will . . . continue to serve as a justification for an exploitation of our resources which in many cases is tantamount to robbery . . . Under a pretence of friendship and co-operation, they manage to make our administration share their guilt as plunderers and oppressors."[2]

In retrospect, the amazing thing is that it took almost five years for many NS leaders to reach this conclusion. The German attitude towards Quisling had at least been fairly consistent. Hitler used him when he could be useful, and otherwise he ignored him, without bothering much about the courtesy nominally due to a fellow "leader". The more Quisling's political weightlessness became apparent, the more openly this German attitude was revealed.

1 OPA, Quisling dossier, letter Prytz–Quisling.
2 Institute of History, Oslo University, Støren Papers.

MOBILISATION FOR GERMANY?

During Quisling's brief period of relative optimism at the beginning of 1942, he prepared a memorandum intended to serve as a point of departure for future negotiations which included a chapter on "co-operation" with the German *Wehrmacht*.[1] According to this, Norway was voluntarily to place at the disposal of the Reich such ports and airfields as were necessary "for the common defence and for offensive warfare, since the navy and the air force in the future Germanic union will be one federal and common Germanic navy and air force". Coastal defences and army forces were to remain under Norwegian command. Although this arrangement was seen as a post-war aim, it should be prepared already during the war. "It would be desirable, by making use of the existing constitutional rules on compulsory military service, to start immediately with the organisation of a Norwegian army corps consisting of three divisions . . ."

In 1943 Quisling then began seriously considering a regular mobilization of Norwegians, and discussed this repeatedly and officially with SS *Obersturmbannführer* Neumann, who was then head of the section of the *Reichskommissariat* that immediately supervised *Nasjonal Samling*.[2] Quisling suggested a mobilization of 50,000 men to be used on the eastern front against the Russians. In a lengthy written answer of 18 December 1943, Neumann turned down the suggestion. He listed a long series of counter-arguments of a technical, military and political nature. It would *inter alia* prove impossible to organise the call-up, the necessary transportation and housing. Those mobilised would probably escape to Sweden and there constitute a direct invitation to the Allies to carry out an invasion. The Quisling régime would be left with an outstanding fiasco, and whatever sympathy still existed for Germany would be lost for ever. Neumann's answer was composed in slightly, and sometimes openly, ironical terms: even were Quisling to mobilise 50,000 men, the first thing he would need would be another

1 OPA, Quisling dossier.
2 *Ibid.*

50,000 reliable men to go and bring them in. These 50,000 men were obviously not available.

Thus, the idea of carrying out a mobilisation had been put forward by the NS, and turned down by the Germans of the *Reichskommissariat*. It did, however, turn up again. Reasoning from somewhat different premises, "Minister of Justice" Riisnæs had already advocated total or partial mobilisation in Norway to provide troops for the eastern front. But Riisnæs was closer to the German SS, and on 17 January 1944 submitted his suggestion to, among others, SS General Gottlob Berger, a near associate of Himmler, particularly in questions concerning "Germanic volunteers". Riisnæs' letter included a programme for the mobilisation of five classes, about 75,000 men, to be carried out with the assistance of German civilian and military authorities. The frontiers would have to be sealed as well as the coastline, and those who did not report themselves at once would be collected. Norwegian recruits were then to be dispersed in German units, where they were always to be in a minority.[1]

Some time after these suggestions had been made Quisling visited Germany, where he was received by both Himmler and Hitler. Quisling then again brought up both his blueprints for a common Germanic defence organisation after the war and the idea of a Norwegian mobilisation as soon as possible. He had in mind three Norwegian divisions for use outside occupied Norway. But Hitler, who usually made a point of receiving Terboven first and alone, seeing Quisling afterwards together with Terboven and others, this time left it to the *Reichskommissar* to turn down the suggestion with arguments similar to those of Neumann.

As the final catastrophe approached, Quisling became increasingly absorbed by ever more fantastic ideas, such as his scheme of "offering Norwegian citizenship" to the German army in Norway, some 350,000 men. During the final weeks of the war Quisling also seems to have believed that his *Hird* formations would be allowed to assume responsibility for public order in the transition period, together with the "Home Forces"

1 OPA, Riisnæs dossier.

of the resistance movement. When this suggestion was made at an NS meeting, one of Quisling's "ministers" reported that there was no discussion as to the political possibility of the plan, only some speculation as to what kind of insignia would have to be designed for their uniforms.[1] It is hardly fair to hold Quisling entirely responsible for all this wishful thinking—if thinking it was—in the very last phase of the drama. But it nevertheless represents a comprehensible point of culmination in the development of a man who from the outset was so conspicuously devoid of a sense of realism.

NAZIFICATION—GENTLE OR VIOLENT

Presumably, Quisling had a fair chance of proving his worth during the first six months following September 1940. If so, he was entirely unable to profit from the opportunity. In actual fact, he paid little attention to everyday politics in Norway, and considered the political future of occupied Norway and his place therein as a matter to be decided between the two statesmen involved, Hitler and himself. If he could have his peace treaty and organise his "government", the remaining problems would solve themselves.

This opinion was by no means shared by his supporters. Many of them found it more necessary to work out what they frequently referred to as constructive policies, without pushing Gleichschaltung too fast or demanding an immediate formal "government" status. The discussion was summed up in 1940-41 in the two slogans of "the brief line" and "the long line".

Short or long, the lines converged in a future national-socialist state under the auspices of Nasjonal Samling, but opinion was divided about the best practical procedure. Should the assault on "the old system" be in the form of a short and violent offensive, or a drawn-out period of patient pressure and persuasion? Spokesmen for the "long line", among them the two "Commissioner Ministers" Meidell and Irgens, wanted to act carefully and slowly in many respects, avoiding difficult conflicts, showing their strength and ability in constructive policies as far as

1 OPA, Skarphagen dossier.

possible, and keeping well within the scope left to them by the Germans, without compromising national-socialist ideology.[1] In situations of acute conflict they frequently preferred less drastic solutions. The more impatient quarters wanted to achieve as much as possible as soon as possible, *"sich durchsetzen"* as Quisling himself used to quote from the German. For instance, existing institutions should be taken over rapidly and placed under the control of reliable persons, using violence if needed. If this policy could be carried out systematically, the "new order" would be introduced from the top both in government and in social stratification generally. In other words, their policy was to appoint reliable "leaders" and have them build, as it were, a foundation for leadership underneath themselves step by step.

Quisling settled for the "short line", if he perceived of any choice at all. This was his way in politics, based on a concept of political organisation as a matter of command and obedience, where political change was effected by placing new men at the top and expecting others to submit. He was unable to imagine the strength of the forces bound to be released by such a procedure in a traditionally democratic society. He was a true authoritarian. So was Terboven in his manner, but he had a sense of political dynamics which Quisling did not possess. When Terboven suggested a strengthening of the party, so that it would in due time be able to support a government, Quisling could not help turning the whole reasoning upside down. For him the diametrically opposed policy seemed obvious: allow the NS to have its government, and then the party would grow stronger. In the face of German opposition, he frequently argued that Norwegians had a tradition of "obedience to the law". If his government was given a legal status by the Germans, Norwegians would obey. The Germans, who knew more about totalitarian politics, were both amused and annoyed.

In his policy of trying to take over from the top without bothering about the foundation, Quisling was actively and aggressively supported by Hagelin. This became evident immediately after Quisling's partial comeback in September 1940, and

1 OPA, Meidell and Irgens dossiers.

marked the beginning of a long series of notorious failures. Attempts to combine such a take-over policy with a strategy of "divide and rule" collapsed when confronted with the strong feeling of solidarity and unity that formed the psychological background for Norwegian resistance from 1940 onwards. The "sports front" provides a typical illustration. Since 1924, organised sport in Norway had been split along a mainly political line, with a workers' sports association closely associated with labour. At the outbreak of the Second World War, serious attempts were made by both sides to bridge the gap, and in the months following the campaign in Norway these negotiations proceeded with surprising smoothness. Early in September formal unification was a fact.

On the day when *Reichskommissar* Terboven proclaimed the "Council of Commissioner Ministers", German police arrested the former officers of the workers' sports association. Simultaneously, the Quisling régime appointed a "Minister for Sport" and announced its intention to organise the whole movement on the German pattern with appointed political commisioners. The new "minister" soon made the mistake of trying to play on the previous antagonism between the organisations, and by so doing succeeded in uniting them against himself. In a conference with the "minister" they demanded that propaganda and political interference of any kind should be banished from Norwegian sports. A representative of the "ministry" vainly retorted that work for *Nasjonal Samling* was not political propaganda, as the NS was not a political party but a movement.[1] When it became obvious that the appointment of commissioners was being prepared, and when on 4 November the "ministry" ordered all branch organisations to cancel their regular annual meetings, an open clash was unavoidable. The whole central committee then resigned, with the result that for the rest of the war normal activities in athletics, football, winter-sports, etc. was reduced to a poor compromise between not quite nothing and almost something. Holmenkollen, for instance, saw no ski-jumping competition during those five years.

Similar techniques were adopted in government, both in the

[1] Cf. *Norges Krig*, Vol. II. p. 620.

central and in the regional administration. The latter is traditionally of particular importance in Norway, stemming directly from the democratic reforms of the first half of the 19th century. Since then local self-government has been one of the main features of Norwegian democracy.

Hagelin, who had taken charge of the Ministry of the Interior, chose to launch a frontal attack. He issued a series of orders and regulations designed to give the "minister" complete control over his subordinates, and over such branches of government as came within his sector. The new regulations had two principal aims: to remove potential resisters, and to have them replaced by "reliable" persons. This meant that a number of civil servants and elected local officials had to be discharged and their successors appointed from above according to the Führer-principle—now described as the "principle of responsibility". Within a month this principle was systematically applied. In October 1940, Hagelin decided that all such bodies as were normally elected and organised under the laws of local self-government should be subject to appointment by the "ministry". Mayors were dismissed, and with them municipal councils and elected bodies and officials of all descriptions. New elections were not to be held, and the "Council of Commissioner Ministers" was authorised to appoint successors.

The same procedure was adopted for all positions under the Ministry of Justice that are normally filled through elections, and also in education, where the main target became the local school councils, always very important in the administration of education in Norway. A newly appointed "chief inspector of schools" made a tour in the Oslo region and issued progress reports to the press on how many councils had been dismissed: eleven as of 11 December and eight more in the following three days. The "Ministry of Church and Education" instructed schools to "introduce pupils to the ideas of the new era in general and about the programme and aims of the NS in particular".[1] New text books were being prepared, and teachers would be required to teach "Christianity and national-socialism".

1 War Collection, Oslo University, Institute of History.

THE TEST OF STRENGTH

The abolition of local self-government and elections released a veritable counter-campaign on the general theme: "Refuse to co-operate". In many towns and villages it proved impossible to find NS members or sympathizers to replace the elected representatives. In such cases Hagelin resigned himself to appointing someone who had previously held such office. Of the numerous protests which followed, one was particularly noteworthy: "I have been informed of my appointment to the office of mayor of Bolsøy. As matters stand, I can refer to none of the grounds listed for refusal. Nor do I refer to the fact that I, for years, have had nothing to do with local government, as I am fully aware that people are being appointed who know much less about it. That 99 % of the local population are against the New Order is not particularly remarkable of Bolsøy, as the proportion is practically the same in the whole country. But as a member of the dismissed and slandered Storting. I consider it improper to assume a function where the prerequisite must be to undermine the rights and the institutions which I, as a representative of the people, was elected to protect."[1]

In December 1940 the nation's legal institutions also refused to co-operate. A judge of the Supreme Court was arrested for "political activities directed against the state". As the Supreme Court subsequently pronounced that the new measures of the régime put an end to the independence of the courts and therefore were unconstitutional as well as inadmissible according to international law, Terboven decided to remove the judges indirectly through lowering the age of retirement by five years. Realising what was to come, the Court anticipated his next move, and stated that if they were denied their constitutional right of judicial review they would have to resign. Deadlock was reached, and a supreme court of the "new order" was then appointed, manned by NS supporters.

Numerous examples could be quoted to show how the frontal attack on democratic institutions only served to demonstrate to what extent the NS was incapable of replacing the old system.

[1] Reprinted in several clandestine newspapers at the time.

A radio operator from the Home Forces in activity in the mountains.

Frequently mayors had to be allowed to continue their functions and were able to retain control of important sectors of local affairs. This is true not only of small municipalities; Norway's second city Bergen had its old mayor until March 1942. Speaking generally, party members or sympathizers were appointed wherever it seemed at all possible, regardless of qualifications. Nevertheless, the NS was only able to supply candidates for a minority of public offices. A survey of how far the régime had been able to carry out the political infiltration of the school councils up to the spring of 1942 shows a national average of 18 per cent.[1] In other words, only every fifth council member was an NS man. Thus, in spite of the virtually complete powers of appointment, the NS never managed to acquire control of this important sector—mainly for want of suitable candidates.

Again and again this pattern repeated itself, whenever it came to a test of strength between Quisling's "new order" and the old one. This was Quisling's decisive defeat, and the real victory of resistance in Norway. And as far as the Germans were concerned, Quisling was not a hesitant, reluctant or refractory national-socialist, merely a useless one. The compactness of the

1 *Om Landssvikoppgjøret,* p. 30.

front against Quisling and his régime no doubt has a negative explanation: the odium that attached to his partnership with the enemy, and the fact that he was made a scapegoat, even beyond his responsibilities, for hardships, sufferings, injustice, violence, and such things as war entails. And then also resistance, like its enemy, had its fellow-travellers. In fact, being so overwhelmingly superior in numbers, it probably had more of them.

No responsible resistance leader in Norway is likely to romanticise or exaggerate by describing Norway as a nation of resisters. Memories of hesitation, timidity and a safety-first attitude would be far too vivid for him to do so. Such idealizing as has occurred originated from other quarters. Nevertheless, it is safe to say that even in the periods of hardest stress, the overwhelming majority of Norwegians rallied around resistance, not because each and every Norwegian was a democratic superman, but because the active kernel of convinced and dedicated partisans of democracy was numerous and resolute enough to exert a social pressure which was felt all the way from the very centres of resistance to the most obvious fence-sitters.

Norwegian resistance was fortunate also in its exceptional unity. There was in Norway one co-ordinated, unified civilian branch, and one co-ordinated, highly centralised, military branch of resistance. That was all: there were no competing organisations. An exception might be made for communist groups, but it does not go very far. At the end of the war the communist groups—neither very strong nor very numerous—were effectively subordinated to the general organisation of the resistance. There was co-operation at the top between the military and the civilian branches, and also between resistance leaders and the Government in London. "Milorg", or the military resistance organisation, was recognised by the Government at the end of 1941 as the fourth arm of defence, and the civilian leadership issued directions to guide the population's attitude and conduct, and had these broadcast by the Government through the Norwegian broadcasting service in London.

This unity of command and execution reflected the general identity of purpose. In few if any other occupied territories did resistance work so exclusively and with such general support towards a simple restitution, a restoration of affairs to their normal state before the German invasion. No successful attempt was made to combine the aims of resistance with programmes of fundamental reform or of change. There was an overwhelming loyalty towards the traditional system, and a confidence that future problems could find their solution within the familiar framework of democratic institutions. Quisling was never able to shake this general conviction and loyalty.

QUISLING AND HIS ROLE

The part of Vidkun Quisling in this story has been described in many different ways. Some see him as a hero, a visionary, a man of the 21st century working among petty nationalists of the 18th and victimised by them. Others have felt that a man whose political career is to this extent compromised by treason and violence must also be immoral as a private person. These are partisan views. Partisans on both sides are moreover apt to proclaim their confidence in a future "judgement of history" which they assume will endorse their own opinions. Historians think differently.

Normally, historians must resign themselves to the discussion of problems for which the available material provides plausible answers. If they feel that every man is a universe in himself, they also realise that they are poorly equipped to penetrate into the mysteries of human behaviour. They are likely to distrust the simple-explanation theories; the relationship between a man's mind and his politics is to them an intricately involved one, without simple answers. For the same reason there are few simple questions that really make sense. For instance, the question whether Quisling was a "good man", implicated more or less deservedly in "bad politics", does not necessarily open up a line of valid or even interesting historical reasoning.

A study of Quisling as a politician seems more rewarding, and it is anything but a success story. At the outset he placed himself in an impossible situation by involving himself with the German aggression both before and after 9 April 1940. Subsequently he was unable to extricate himself, and equally unable to change his alliances. He chose to remain chained to totalitarian policies of which he claimed to have disapproved. He was unable to develop constructive policies, and therefore became a burden even to those on whose side he fought. He never had a strong, or even fully developed, sense of political reality, and as the war went on he receded into a world of his own.

A man of few, simple and fairly primitive ideas on politics, he nevertheless deduced from them a line of political conduct. This is where his political ability ended. It took him to the borderline of practical politics, but no further. When it came to political action in a given setting, as soon as analysis, calculation, estimates and manoeuvering were required, he was helpless.

This appears immediately in his way of interpreting political situations. He made use only of loose and wide abstractions, and significant details, facts and dates therefore remained unnoticed unless they were tied in with his own set of general notions. This was hardly a conscious process. He did not deliberately ignore or rise over what he held to be petty considerations or unimportant facts. It seems rather as if these things did not exist in his mind; as if his political perception was incapable of seizing them. He was dedicated to the building of theoretical structures and the definition of general aims in general terms, but was unable to work out the simple problems of everyday conflict or co-operation with his political surroundings.

This is one aspect of the so-called riddle of Vidkun Quisling. Friends and enemies approach him from different quarters, consequently some see him as a political prophet, others as a political nullity. Some see him as a man with his eyes turned to the stars, others find him ignorant of the ground on which he trod. A study of his politics can hardly fail to support the latter view. He projected his vagueness into a political world of which he knew little, and of which he had no desire to learn more. Thus, for instance, he declared during his trial that his view on Russia was a by-product of his passion for his fatherland. Russia was in reality a greater Norway, had been founded by Norwegians and populated by "our ancestors". He went on to say: "This was my point of departure in my estimate of Russian conditions . . . I have not changed my point of view in these matters. Circum-

92

stances have altered, I have not."[1] Such rigidity has not much in common with seriousness of purpose. In politics at least it seems more like immobility bordering on lameness.

This does not mean that Quisling did nothing. His consistent policy of assisting the invader and occupant, and of changing the constitution by unconstitutional means, was accompanied by a series of attempts to build in "new Norway" institutions similar to those of Hitler's Germany. The Quisling régime had its own *Hird,* organised on the model of the German SA; its own SS; its own political police and political prisons; its *Volksgerichtshof* or "people's court"; its informers and its torturers. With it all there was also the secrecy and the lack of control typical of the "principle of responsibility" where so many hands did not know what the other ones were doing.

Certainly, many of those approximately 1⅓ % of the Norwegian population who joined the party never saw the most incriminating aspects of native Nazism in Norway, and still can not bring themselves to believe it. On the other hand, re-reading the party papers *Fritt Folk* or *Hirdmannen* or *Germaneren* is still a shocking experience. But those who echoed Adolf Hitler when he was still in power are nowadays silent, and their recorded voices are mostly heard by those who in the past used to close their ears against them.

What then of Vidkun Quisling himself and his "riddle"? This man, whose name gave us a new word for traitor, became the best known of fifth column leaders in a period marked by many strange deviations in political allegiance. Outside his native country he is hardly known to history except as a symbol, and therefore he continues to lend himself to widely different interpretations. Because the man himself is so shadowy a figure to the outside world, the lapse of time makes it easy for revelations of his private qualities to confound the issue of his political turpitude.

In Norway, on the other hand, the outline of his personal character is widely known and much of it was brought in evidence at his trial in 1945. He was an awkward and rather shy man, given to long monologues and equally long silences, mainly because he was a person of few and rather vague general ideas,

1 *Straffesak mot V. Quisling,* p. 459.

taking little or no interest in other people unless they came to sit at his feet. He had excellent manners, frugal habits, and a marked disinclination for any personal extravagance. His scholastic record was outstanding; in fact, he graduated from the Military Academy with the highest honours ever awarded. There was hardly a trace of any love of violence or dishonest tendencies in any part of his life outside his activities in politics.

Because of this startling contrast between Quisling's private and public life, attempts have indeed been made to explain away the latter. Could it not be that he was a victim of circumstances, an honest man chained to the Nazi juggernaut; or a visionary who looked beyond a fratricidal war to the supranational community of the future but who, by an accident of history, had happened to choose the wrong partner?

However, there is no need for such attempts to add a kind of mental fourth dimension to one who was undoubtedly well-bred and intellectually well endowed, but who in his sum total of qualities and shortcomings nevertheless was a rather ordinary sort of person. For one of the terrifying things about Nazism was its ability to attract just such a type.

The entanglement with Nazi aggression lifted Quisling out of political insignificance into a new dimension where he was entirely out of his depth. The sequel was his six-day ministry at the start of the German invasion, then two years of ham-fisted management from behind the scenes, and finally the three years of office as *Minister-President*.

The last months of the war were bitter ones for the dwindling group of the faithful. Quisling's thoughts seem to have wandered far beyond the borderline which divides mere wishful thinking from the absolutely fantastic. At one moment he saw himself as a head of state who had served his country for five years—as long, he said, as the viking king Olav Trygvason (995–1000)—and served it well; but at other moments he must have sensed deeply the bitterness of "Minister" Støren's remarks on the authorities of the Third Reich: "Under a pretence of friendship and co-operation, they managed to make our administration share their guilt as plunderers and oppressors."

Having shared the guilt, Quisling shared the punishment.

Norway in Exile

THE SITUATION

The operations in Norway against the German invaders formally ended on 10 June 1940 when a representative of the Norwegian High Command signed an agreement providing for the capitulation of the remaining armed forces in northern Norway. At that time, however, King Haakon, Prime Minister Nygaardsvold and the Government were on the high seas making their way to Britain and exile; with them sailed the remainder of the Norwegian navy—about a dozen vessels and four hundred officers and other ranks—and a small number of officers and other ranks from the army and the air force.

The purpose of their departure from Norwegian territory had been recorded in a proclamation from the King and the Government dated 7 June. After stating the reasons why it had become pointless to continue the struggle on Norwegian soil, this document declared that the King and his Government had accepted the advice of the High Command to this effect, and had decided to leave the national territory.

"However," the proclamation continued, "they do not therefore abandon the struggle to regain Norway's independence. On the contrary—it will be carried on outside the country's borders. They have the firm hope that the German assailants will soon be forced to relinquish their booty, and that the Norwegian people, together with other peoples now suffering under the German yoke, shall again have their right and their freedom.

In this period of struggle, Norway's King and Government will be the free spokesmen for the national claims of the Norwegian people. They will to the utmost possible extent maintain the sovereign existence of the Norwegian Kingdom, in order that none of the rights pertaining to a free state shall go by default. It will be their task to defend the status and political rights of the country and its people, in such a way that the nation in the hour of victory can step forth and assert its national freedom."

By this proclamation, and its solemn pledge to stake everything on the effort to maintain Norway's sovereign status and the endeavour to regain the country's freedom and independence, the objective was set. The Government's constitutional position was also secure, as confirmed by the last free meeting of the Storting on 9 April through the "Elverum Mandate". By that decision the Storting empowered the Government "to be the guardian of the nation's interests and on behalf of Storting and Government to carry out the decisions and measures considered necessary for the country's security and future, until such time as the Government and the President of the Storting after consultation shall call the next ordinary meeting of the Storting."[1] But the outlook in the summer of 1940 was bleak, and the question "How?" was in all minds. In spite of the wide mandate given to the Government, and the tower of firmness and strength provided in the person of King Haakon, the Government's authority needed constant re-assertion. It was needed abroad for the purpose of obtaining recognition from allied and neutral powers as the only legal Norwegian Government. As it turned out, this was achieved without serious difficulties apart from the rather special case of relations with the French Vichy régime. On an entirely different level, however, was the problem of maintaining the Government's authority against German and collaborationist Norwegian efforts to discredit it in the eyes of the people of occupied Norway—efforts aimed at supplanting the legal Government by a régime that would co-operate with Germany.

Events in Norway during the summer and early autumn of 1940, reviewed elsewhere, gave rise to well-founded fears that the Government's failure to keep the country out of war or to defend its neutrality, the subsequent defeat of the Norwegian forces, and the insufficiency of the Allied help, would combine to foster despair and a desire to seek a *modus vivendi* with the German occupiers. Those fears reached a climax with the letter from parliamentary leaders in June 1940 urging the King

1 *UK Report,* p. 114

96

The King speaks to Norway from a BBC studio in London.

to abdicate. But the King's reply, broadcast from London on 8 July, clarified the position by stating that since this proposal was not the result of free deliberation it could in no way relinquish the King from his duty to the Norwegian Constitution. Nor could it release the Government from the mandate which it had received from a free Parliament on 9 April.

This declaration had important effects as an affirmation of the King's position as a leader and rallying point for those who resisted the insidious attempts to establish a nazi régime in Norway, and it also strengthened the Government's position in the efforts to organise Norway's resources for the coming struggle on the side of Britain and the Allies. But this strengthened position was a bond on the future, whose value would depend on the success of the Government's endeavour. Although the tasks that lay ahead might seem so difficult as to be almost overwhelming, the assets at hand were not negligible. First of all, the adventurous but successful transportation of the Bank of Norway's gold reserves through a war-ridden country and then to Britain secured free Norway's financial independence, at least in the short run. In the long run, economic solvency was to be assured by the Government's most important single resource: the Norwegian merchant navy.

NORWAY'S CONTRIBUTION

With the merchant navy's pre-war size of almost five million tons, amounting to about seven per cent of the world's total tonnage, Norway ranked fourth among the shipping nations. Moreover, its ships were modern and fast, and the fleet had a large proportion of tankers—every fifth of the world's tankers was Norwegian. The importance of this asset in war-time was realised by the Norwegian Government from the beginning, and as early as on 22 April 1940 a provisional decree laid the foundation for the Government's increasingly complete control over the merchant navy. The value of the fleet was, of course, no less evident to Germany, and one of the first acts of the Quisling "government" on 10 April was to request all captains of Norwegian vessels to proceed to Norwegian, German or neutral harbours and await further instructions. Not a single captain, however, heeded the request, and only the one-sixth of the fleet which was within the reach of the Germans came under their control.

During April and May, Norwegian shipowners in London, in co-operation with the Government, took the first steps to organise what became known as "Nortraship"—the Norwegian Shipping and Trade Mission. From the beginning it was the biggest shipping company in the world. It still was when the war ended, although by then almost half its 1940 tonnage had been lost. Throughout the war, while the dispositions of the fleet were naturally decided in close consultation with Britain and the other Allies, the Norwegian flag on each of the fleet's vessels was both symbol and living reality. And the freight

(Left:) A stoker on a Norwegian merchant ship in Atlantic convoy. (Right:) One of the old Norwegian transport vessels beached on the Normandy coast with supplies for the invasion armies.

incomes of the merchant navy prevented Norway from becoming a debtor and financial liability to the Allies.

However, and in spite of the valuable contribution of the merchant navy to the Allied war effort, it seemed an essential task of the Government to establish that Norway would also be a fighting ally, with armed forces that could play a role, however small, in the common struggle and also eventually be the spearhead of a liberation force for Norway. The modest beginnings of Norwegian forces could be seen in the training camp in Scotland and in the personnel and the naval vessels that followed the Government into exile. The Norwegian navy had the best starting position, with fifteen vessels in readiness or being equipped for service by mid-summer. By the autumn four ships were thus serving in Iceland under the operational control of the British Admiral Commanding Iceland, doing patrol duty in the Arctic Ocean. The first entirely new vessels acquired by the Norwegian navy were two motor torpedo-boats, ordered from British ship-yards before the war, which began their duties on 2 July in the English Channel as a Norwegian sub-division of the 11th MTB-Flotilla. Other ships then began serving as soon as they could be equipped and manned. From 1940 to

1945, 118 naval vessels at one time or another sailed under the Norwegian flag. A survey as of 1 January 1943 shows 58 vessels on active service performing widely differing duties, from patrol service in the Arctic Ocean to minesweeping in the Persian Gulf.[1]

The Norwegian air force had to look far afield for training grounds and planes, but in the autumn of 1940 about 120 officers and other ranks could begin their training at the newly established "Little Norway" training centre in Toronto, Canada. New recruits were also coming in, and on 25 April 1941 the first operational Norwegian air squadron was established in Iceland, equipped with Northrop seaplanes which had been ordered from America before the war. Serving as 330 (Norwegian) Squadron under RAF Coastal Command, their tasks included convoy duty and anti-submarine patrols in the North Atlantic. From 1943 this squadron was equipped with Sunderland flying boats and stationed on Shetland, where their duties covered an area from the coast of northern Norway to the Azores and Iceland.

The first Norwegian fighter squadron was established late in 1941 as 331 (N) Squadron, and was joined in January 1942 by 332 (N) Squadron. For a long period, the fighters were stationed at North Weald outside London, and took their full share in establishing Allied air superiority over southern England and the Channel. In 1943, 331 Squadron in fact led all the Allied squadrons in the number of enemy planes destroyed. In the spring of 1943, 333 (N) Squadron came into being, when a flight of Catalina flying boats was joined by a recently formed flight of Mosquito fighter-bombers. Stationed in Scotland, the Catalinas and Mosquitoes performed duties which involved them in frequent operations over Norwegian territory.

Because of the comparatively rapid development of the navy and the air force, and the need for sailors for the merchant navy, the Government was soon faced with a growing scarcity of personnel. Although many Norwegians abroad volunteered for the armed services, and a number of recruits came across the North Sea from Norway, this was not enough and the

1 Steen, *Norges Sjøkrig*, Vol. V (Oslo 1959), p. 76 and 218.

(Left:) A signalman of the Royal Norwegian Navy. (Right:) A Norwegian submarine loading provisions for another patrol.

Government had to find other sources of recruitment. A first step had been taken in the summer of 1940 with the registration of Norwegian citizens of military age living in Britain. However, the complexities of the jurisdictional problems that were entailed in exercising legal authority in a foreign country delayed the actual conscription of Norwegians on British soil until the end of 1940.

On the other hand, even after the question of recruitment had come some way towards solution, the intricate problem of priorities in allotting personnel to the various services had to be resolved. A strong case could be made out for according first priority to the needs of the merchant navy, which constituted Norway's most valuable contribution to the cause of the Allies. In the summer of 1940, moreover, the prospect of a German attempt to invade Britain, as well as the vital task of assuring that the supplies carried by the merchant vessels actually reached the British Isles, created an urgent need for naval personnel to man the vessels that patrolled the approaches to Britain, The British navy was ready to provide the ships as long as the Norwegian navy could man them.

During the summer and autumn of 1940, therefore, this led to a number of recruits being transferred to the navy from the army training camp in Scotland. When the air force began to call for recruits in the autumn, the drain on the already severely tapped manpower resources of the new Norwegian army assumed serious proportions. Without denying the strong claims of immediate priority for the other services, since the army was working on a more long-term basis, the Army Command stressed the need for stable conditions that would enable them to plan the building up of land forces. Some measure of stability was achieved later, but the army inevitably remained low on the lists of priorities, and the initial goal of an army of 2,500 men was not reached until 1943. The major part of the land forces was stationed in Scotland throughout the war as part of the home defences of the British Isles, while being trained for participation in the liberation of Norway. Smaller garrisons were from time to time posted to Norwegian possessions in the Arctic and Antarctic, and one company was kept in Iceland for the larger part of the war. From the forces in Scotland were also recruited the men who served in the special company for secret operations in Norway, mentioned below, and the Norwegian troop of No. 10 (Inter-Allied) Commando.

THE NATURE OF THE ALLIANCE

One major question that soon arose was the formal nature of Norway's co-operation with the Allies. This involved both the over-all character of the Alliance and, on the more practical level, the arrangement of Norway's military contribution and the pattern of military and naval co-operation. While it would have been unrealistic of the Norwegian Government to expect a measurable share in the supreme direction of the war, since responsibility both for formulation and execution of strategy had evidently to rest with the British, still a basis had to be found for a collaboration which safeguarded purely Norwegian interests without reducing the effectiveness of Norway's contribution to the common struggle.

In the summer of 1940 a preliminary statement of the principles of co-operation was put on paper, in the form of a Norwegian memorandum to the British Government which laid down the pattern for the first year of co-operation.[1] In so far as the new Norwegian army was concerned, the intention was that

[1] NRV (Den Norske Regjerings Virksomhet under krigen fra 9 april 1940 til 22 juni 1945), Vol. IV (Oslo, 1948), pp. 217–219.

(Left:) A Norwegian "Mosquito» fighter-bomber between sorties. (Right:) A "Catalina" flying boat of the R.N.A.F. in drifting ice near Reykjavik, Iceland.

it should participate in the defence of Great Britain together with the British forces. It would further, when the time was ripe, participate in actions and operations intimately connected with the re-conquest of Norway. The Norwegian air force, when ready for action, would constitute Norwegian squadrons with their own planes and Norwegian personnel, but would fight side by side with Allied squadrons. With regard to the more immediately important question of the navy, Norwegian and Norwegian-manned vessels would serve under British operational control in the defence of the British Isles and, in so far as the vessels were suitable, in operations against the enemy off the coasts of Norway.

The British Government was in general agreement with these initial terms of reference, and Norwegian forces could then begin training and operating together with the British. A formal and detailed agreement "in respect of the Norwegian Armed Forces in the United Kingdom" was subsequently negotiated and signed on 28 May 1941. The preamble to this agreement stated the determination of both countries to prosecute the war to a successful conclusion, and also confirmed "that one of the objects of the war is the re-establishment of the freedom and independence of Norway through its complete liberation from German domination".[1] Article one re-affirmed the two-fold purpose of setting up the Norwegian forces abroad as being participation in the defence of the British Isles and the liberation of Norway, and stated that the Norwegian forces would for this purpose be "organised and employed under British command, in its character as the Allied High Command, as the Armed Forces of the Kingdom of Norway allied with the United Kingdom". The agreement further specified that the Norwegian Government would bear all the expenses of the Norwegian armed forces.

In the terms of a specific section dealing with land forces, the Norwegian troops were to "retain the character of a Norwegian force in respect of personnel, particularly as regards discipline, language, promotion and duties". The units and formations were also to be commanded by Norwegian officers, subject to the above-mentioned reservation about the Allied command of superior formations. A corresponding section about the navy stated that units of the Norwegian navy would be commanded by Norwegian officers, and would remain a Norwegian administrative and financial responsibility, but that vessels were to be attached to the British navy under British operational control. Similar regulations were contained in a special section concerning the air force.

That the Norwegian Government went so far in subordinating its forces to Allied operational control reflected both the confidence felt towards the senior partner in the Alliance, and the realisation that coalition warfare is a rigorously organised and highly centralised affair, where efficiency must often overrule considerations of national susceptibilities and preferences. The same combination of confidence and practical realism was present in the Government's attitude at the more general level of foreign policy. The guiding lines for this policy were first publicly enunciated in a speech which Trygve Lie, then acting Foreign Minister, gave through the BBC in December 1940. He stressed the close ties binding Norway to the West, primarily to the United Kingdom, but also

[1] English and Norwegian texts of this Agreement in *NRV*, Vol. IV, pp. 220–245.

The King and the Crown Prince reviewing units of the Norwegian Brigade in Scotland after field manœuvres.

to the United States and other sea-faring nations. It was Norway's aim to strengthen those ties through war-time co-operation, thereby laying the foundations for continued close collaboration after the war in the pursuit of their common aim of liberty and security. For this purpose, hopes and plans were not enough: it required an active Norwegian contribution to the wartime Alliance whose aim was also the liberation of Norway from alien rule.[1]

A further and more formal expression of Norway's will to co-operate with its partners in the Alliance came in the first Declaration of St. James's Palace of 12 June 1941, when the Norwegian Government joined thirteen other nations in solemnly declaring their mutual aid and assistance in the struggle against the common enemies. When Germany a few days later attacked the Soviet Union, the Norwegian Government supported Churchill's policy of offering the support of the Alliance to any nation fighting against nazism. In August, Norway and

1 Lie, *Med England i Ildlinjen* (Oslo 1956), pp. 118—120.

the Soviet Union then resumed regular diplomatic relations. Moreover, public statements on Norway's foreign policy thereafter introduced the idea of Norway as a bridge-builder between the U.S.S.R. and the Western Allies. In November 1941, an article by Trygve Lie in *The Times* once more stressed the value of the co-operation undertaken in war-time, and expressed Norway's hope that the resulting unity of purpose, particularly among the four great powers of the United Kingdom, the United States, China and the Soviet Union, would also afford a basis for intimate co-operation after the war.[1] On later occasions as well, particularly the solemn Declaration of the United Nations signed in Washington on 1 January 1942, Norway and the other participating nations, now numbering 26 including the U.S.S.R., declared their agreement with the principles of Roosevelt's and Churchill's Atlantic Charter of the previous autumn, and pledged all their military and economic resources to the common effort to defeat the enemy.

On several occasions in the early years of the war, the Norwegian Government expressed its willingness to consider regional forms of co-operation after the war, in the military and economic fields. Such co-operation was then envisaged among the countries bordering on the North Sea and the Atlantic Ocean. When at one stage the idea of a Nordic bloc was put forward, the Norwegian Government, while agreeing to the obvious desirability of close co-operation with its Scandinavian neighbours, rejected the suggestion of such a bloc as being too narrow in scope and therefore not in accordance with Norway's true interests. Thoughts of a continental European bloc were also rejected as an unsatisfactory solution to the post-war needs of Norway as a nation with a maritime and Atlantic outlook.

In the later years of the war, however, this "Atlantic" scheme for a regional association naturally receded behind the emerging plans for a universal organisation—the United Nations. And after the proposals from Dumbarton Oaks in 1944 outlining a charter for such a universal organisation, it was clear that the scope which these proposals allowed, for regional co-operation within the framework of the world organisation, removed any

1 *The Times,* 14 November 1941.

A railway bridge blown up by resistance saboteurs to slow down German troop movements.

fundamental contradiction between Norway's desire for Atlantic collaboration and its wholehearted support for a universal system. At the San Francisco conference, where the Charter of the United Nations was finally worked out in the spring of 1945, Norway's participation demonstrated a marked will to compromise on its particular wishes and desires whenever these conflicted with the primary aim of an effective organisation which from the outset would have the active support of the great powers. Unlike many other small nations, which through fear of giving the great powers too free a hand in the settlement of international disputes fought to establish strict safeguards for the principle of national sovereignty, Norway therefore gave its support to extended commitments to an international order for the purpose of a more effective maintenance of peace.

CONTACT WITH NORWAY

Important as the problems of Norway's relations with other nations were, they could never be allowed to overshadow the Government's most crucial concern: its relationship with the

107

Norwegian people. The exiled Government had all the time to keep in mind the danger of becoming a head without a body, a fate which befell some other exiled governments that lost touch with and authority over their peoples in the home countries. While the foundation for the Norwegian Government's continued authority over the people of occupied Norway had been strengthened by the unwavering stand of the King and his Ministers through the summer of 1940, that authority had to be affirmed again and again. For this purpose, lines of communication with the home country were an essential prerequisite, and the initial steps to establish such lines had already been taken. The first war-time Norwegian broadcast from London was heard on 9 April 1940, and from that time onwards the BBC played an increasingly important part in stiffening the morale of the Norwegian people. Through news, special messages to the resistance movement and speeches by Norwegians in London, this broadcasting service promoted the unity between the legal Norwegian authorities and the people in the occupied country, to such an extent that the Germans found it necessary to requisition all wireless sets at the end of 1941.

Personal two-way contact was also established in the summer of 1940 when, on the authority of the Foreign Minister, the first couriers went from England to Norway in order to seek out reliable elements which could form a nucleus for further contact between London and Norway. Other links were established in direct liaison with British intelligence services, for the primary purpose of serving Allied military interests by providing information on German naval movements off the coast of Norway. Beginning that autumn, selected Norwegian personnel in the United Kingdom were recruited for future special operations on Norwegian territory in connection with the emerging resistance organisations in Norway.

Such clandestine tasks were as yet new to Norwegians on both sides of the North Sea, but in spite of set-backs due to inexperience the secret web continued to spread. In 1941 the personnel recruited in Britain for special operations were organised as an independent company under joint Anglo-Norwegian leadership. By the end of the war, practically all of the more than five

A fishing boat arrives at the Shetlands after crossing the North Sea with refugees from the Gestapo.

hundred men of this unit had participated in one or more operations in occupied Norway. For the purpose of co-ordinating the growing network of secret contacts and underground organisations, in close liaison with British agencies engaged in parallel tasks, the Government at the end of 1940 set up its own intelligence bureau in London under the authority of the Ministry of Defence.

An increasing British interest in operations on Norwegian territory became evident when, in March 1941, the first of a series of "hit-and-run" raids was carried out on the Norwegian coast. Norwegian personnel participated in the planning and execution of this and subsequent operations, but British concern for secrecy did not as yet permit an official and close co-operation with the Norwegian Government in such matters. Similarly, the British still showed a preference for working in Norway through a separate underground network, from fear that a widespread and centralised Norwegian resistance organisation outside their control would be too exposed to enemy penetration. From the winter of 1941/42, however, not only did the resistance organisation in Norway accept the subordination of its activities to the authority of the King and the Government, through the newly established Norwegian High Command in London, but a collaboration committee was set up in London to ensure unity of purpose and effort between British and Norwegian agencies engaged in secret operations.

The committee came about partly as a result of two major raids on the Norwegian coast at Christmas time 1941 which in the long run can be seen to have had beneficial effects, but which brought immediate and severe German reprisals against the local population. The Norwegian Government was not a party to the preparation of these raids, and the repercussions led to more insistent, and this time successful, demands for a larger Norwegian share in the planning of such operations.

For the rest of the war a special department of the Norwegian High Command, in close co-operation with the British Special Operations Executive and later also with the American Office of Strategic Services, dealt with the planning and execution of sabotage and other secret operations in Norway in liaison with the military organisation of the Norwegian resistance movement. Norwegian mining and other industries were important to the German war economy, and from a Norwegian point of view it was in most cases better to deprive Germany of those benefits by way of sabotage than by bombing, in order to spare civilian lives. Several successful sabotage actions, notably the destruction of Norsk Hydro's "heavy water" plant and stocks, gave eloquent evidence of the success of this policy.

Although the difficulties of maintaining operational contact with occupied Norway should not be underrated, the country was in a far better position than most of the other occupied territories of Europe. In the early years of the war, the 190 miles of ocean that separate Norway from the British Isles at the narrowest point became an important link between the two countries. At first it was mostly one-way traffic, as recruits for the Norwegian fighting services left for Scotland and the Shetlands

Mortar drill for recruits to the Norwegian police forces in Sweden. The greatest influx of recruits occurred after the Quisling régime in 1944 set about to mobilise Norwegian youth for compulsory labour service. This measure contributed to the numerical strength of the Home Forces as well.

from many scattered points on the Norwegian coast, in fishing boats of all sizes. Later, many of those fishing boats entered the so-called "Shetland bus" service, bringing arms, radios and instructors to Norway, and returning to the United Kingdom with refugees from the Gestapo and agents who had completed their missions. When the Germans intensified their surveillance of the Norwegian coast, however, the fishing boats were no longer adequate for these tasks, and had to be replaced by fast, armed naval vessels. On the other hand, increasing reliance could by then be placed on communications to Norway via Sweden.

The long frontier separating occupied Norway from neutral

Sweden was from the outset an important escape route for refugees from the Gestapo, and very soon Sweden also developed into a convenient meeting-ground between resistance leaders and spokesmen for the Government in London. Through Stockholm also went an increasing part of the correspondence between the Home Front and the Government in exile, as well as much of the intelligence, such as maps and German documents, that could not be transmitted through the many radio stations operated by the resistance in Norway.

Because of the difficulties of transport from Sweden to the United Kingdom, however, since the planes on this route were usually few and far between, Sweden often appeared to be a dead end for refugees from Norway and others who wanted to take an active part in the common struggle. In the first years, moreover, Swedish policy towards Norway and the Norwegians frequently seemed to err on the side of caution and unfriendliness from fear that the Germans might also invade Sweden—an alternative which Norwegians certainly had no reason to relish. But as the tide began to turn against Germany, and Sweden's fears subsided, its policy of neutrality changed perceptibly in Norway's favour. Consequently, during 1943, the Norwegian Government with the co-operation of the Swedish authorities could begin to assemble Norwegians of military age in so-called "Health Camps", where in addition to medical examination and vaccination a certain basic military training of 2—3 weeks duration was given. On an initially modest scale, the training of Norwegian "police reserves" in Sweden likewise began at this time, and from these origins grew what were in fact, but not in theory, regular army units.

PREPARING FOR THE LIBERATION

While the organisation of Norway's contribution to the Allied war effort in general naturally had the highest immediate priority for the Government in exile, the liberation of the home country was the final aim. The establishment, in February 1942, of a Norwegian High Command in London meant that the Norwegians could also begin to take a more active interest in regular military planning for eventual larger operations in Norway. On Churchill's request British military staffs had already started studying the possibility of large-scale operations in Norway, partly for the purpose of opening a second front which might relieve the pressure of the Germans against the Soviet Union and facilitate the transport of essential arms and supplies to the Russian armed forces.[1]

The Norwegian military authorities were now informed of some of the plans that had been considered, and could themselves set to work to ensure that such operations, if ever carried out, would have the benefit of co-operation and advice from those who knew the country, as well as the most up-to-date intelligence from contacts in Norway regarding the enemy's dispositions and establishments. The gathering of intelligence about matters of military and civilian interest from occupied Norway soon became a major task for the Norwegian High Command, although the plans for invading Norway—of which the most advanced was "plan Jupiter" for the seizure of a large part of North Norway, eagerly promoted by Churchill—were to fade behind the more promising prospect of a direct thrust against the heart of the German-dominated continent of Europe.

The Norwegian Government did not actively encourage thoughts of an early invasion of Norway. After mature consideration from a national point of view, the destruction and bloodshed that this would involve could only be justified if the Germans were to embark on a far more severe régime of repression in Norway than had been the case so far. But it was necessary to prepare for all contingencies, and in that connection the role of the Norwegian "Home Front" also had to be assessed and planned. Throughout the war an increasing traffic of arms, equipment and instructors trained in the United Kingdom found its way into Norway, to enable the resistance organisation to carry out its tasks when called upon to do so.

Apart from the operational planning at the military staff level, active preparations were made by the central administration in London for the purpose of safeguarding Norwegian

1 Cf. Gwyer and Butler, *Grand Strategy*, Vol. III (London, 1964) i. a. pp. 203—6 and 646—650.

interests during the process of liberation. In 1943 negotiations began between the Allies and the Norwegian Government for a settlement of the many problems of jurisdiction that would arise during the re-conquest of Norwegian territory. At that time it was impossible to know what form the liberation process would take, and an agreement therefore had to envisage several alternatives. One possibility was that the Germans would capitulate all over Europe at the same time, in which case troops would be sent to Norway mainly for the purpose of ensuring law and order and supervising the peaceful disarmament and internment of the German forces. But it could by no means be discounted that Norway might become the battlefield in an invasion, either to hasten a general German capitulation, or because the German forces in Norway might decide to form a "northern redoubt" and fight on even after the forces in Germany had abandoned the struggle.

Each of these alternatives required a different solution of the division of jurisdiction. In general, however, the final compromise conceded that in the zones of actual fighting, the military commander would need extensive powers also in civil affairs, although he would be assisted by a liaison corps of Norwegian officers. Otherwise the agreement was intended to assure the speediest possible transfer of control to Norwegian political authorities.[1]

For the Norwegians, however, the problems to be considered did not end there. A transfer to civilian authority pre-supposed a network of officials ready to take over at all levels, for the period until normal democratic processes could be restored. In this context a lengthy debate was touched off between the Government and the "Home Front", during which disagreements and misunderstandings did at times arise. Generally, while the members of the Government stressed their natural desire for continuity in the nation's democratic institutions and were anxious to limit any transitional arrangement both in time and scope, the leaders of the resistance were more concerned with devising the most practical and efficient method of ensuring an orderly passage from war to peace. The latter also wished to

[1] Cf. i. a. Donnison, *North-West Europe* (London, 1961)

Constitution Day 1945 in the town of Vadsø in Finnmark, which had been systematically destroyed by the German forces withdrawing from North Norway.

start the post-war period of Norwegian politics with a clean slate on the widest possible basis.

Nevertheless, these differences of opinion did not go very deep, and the result of the debate was that the central council of the resistance movement received wide powers to supervise the period of transition until members of the Government could return to a free Norway. On the whole, Norwegians at home and abroad achieved and maintained throughout a strong unity of purpose, free from the often violent strife about fundamental political aims that marred the war-time history of some other European countries.

The agreement governing civil jurisdiction during the liberation of Norway was signed by the Norwegian and Allied Governments on 16 May 1944. The Soviet Government was also a party to the agreement, and as it turned out the first practical application of its terms came to involve Soviet authorities. After the armistice between the Soviet Union and Finland in September 1944, and the subsequent Finnish declaration of war against Germany, the German forces had to retreat from Finland into northern Norway pursued by the Russian army. The possibility of such a development had been foreseen by the Norwegian Government from the beginning of the year, but only in October, a few days before the first Russian soldiers set foot on Norwegian soil and thereby in fact initiated the liberation of Norwegian territory, did the Soviet Union accept Norway's request to have a Norwegian force participating in that campaign. Not until November 1944 could a hastily organised and necessarily small Norwegian force be sent to Finnmark at the invitation of the Soviet Government.

Even more urgent was the task of sending supplies and food to alleviate the hardship of Norwegian civilians—people who had managed to remain in the area despite the forced evacuation of the population and the subsequent systematic German application of "scorched earth" tactics over the whole province. Energetic Norwegian efforts to provide assistance were made difficult by the tremendous demands on transport and supplies in other, major war theatres—to the bitter disappointment of the Norwegian Government. The supplies that could be sent were however sufficient to prevent starvation, and later in the winter the situation was considerably improved by the air-lift from Sweden of Norwegian police troops, supplies and a field hospital.

Although the Norwegian Government did all in its power to send as many troops as possible to northern Norway in conjunction with the Russian advance into Norwegian territory, this was not a decision that could be lightly taken. There was still a real possibility that forces might be needed in the rest of Norway in the event of a sudden German collapse. Although Allied forces would also be needed, in view of the size of the country and the number of German soldiers to be taken care of, the liberation of Norway had been the essential purpose of weeks and years of training for the men of the Norwegian army, both in Scotland and in Sweden. Together with "Milorg"—the military resistance organisation—they were designed to form the nucleus of the forces needed to ensure an orderly transition from war to peace for the Norwegian nation.

For this reason, against the wishes of the soldiers themselves, the Norwegian land forces had been withheld from participation in the war on the European continent—except for officers doing liaison duty with the Allied forces and special formations that served with the inter-allied commando troops. While units of the Norwegian navy and the fighter squadrons of the Norwegian air force took part in the invasion of Normandy and the subsequent campaign, the soldiers in the army had to be kept in training for an aim that was rapidly approaching but which still to many seemed rather distant. The impatience for action was fully shared by the military resistance organisation in Norway which, apart from occasional sabotage actions sanctioned from London, had to lie low in anticipation of the tasks that awaited them under the liberation. This was a harsh but necessary rule, since any premature action might have jeopardized the plans for later operations and exposed the country to unnecessary reprisals and suffering.

The liberation, on the other hand, had a wider perspective than the passing military and political problems. The restoration of normal conditions in Norway after a German surrender was not only a question of a few hectic days of transition from German to national Norwegian rule, but also of months and years of patient work to eradicate the harmful effects which five years of occupation were bound to have had in practically every sector of the nation's life. This was the main challenge facing the civilian departments of the Norwegian central administration in London, and it was taken in hand as soon as the ministries could acquire a skeleton staff of civil servants. Towards the end of the war, these preparations could also benefit from an exchange of views with resistance leaders in Norway who had concerned themselves with post-war problems. As one of the more urgent tasks, the Norwegian Ministry of Justice in London had from the outset been occupied with the large and complicated work of reviewing the legal apparatus that would bring to justice those who had collaborated in a treasonable

manner with the Germans before and during the occupation—
a matter which will be fully treated in the final chapter.

Another important task was to assure the flow of food and
other supplies to post-war Norway, and to prepare for the
restoration of the country's economy in general, including the
reconstruction of houses and industrial plants and the replacement of run-down machinery: in brief, to re-create a prosperous
Norway. In the autumn of 1942 a new ministry was set up for
these purposes, and its purchases, for the most part made in close
cooperation with the other Allies and with international organisations such as UNRRA, played a major part in laying the foundation for Norway's comparatively quick recovery from the
years of occupation.

For Nortraship and the Norwegian Ministry of Shipping, the
replacement of ships destroyed by German submarines and
mines presented a problem of serious proportions. Not much
help could be expected from the other Allies who would be
facing similar problems regarding their own shipping, but with
the active intervention of the Government a number of con-
tracts for new merchant vessels were concluded with Swedish
ship-builders. This at least ensured the partial restoration of
that vital factor of the Norwegian national economy which
shipping has always constituted.

FROM WAR TO PEACE

By the middle of April 1945, the central parts of western Germany had come under the control of American and British
forces. In a directive from that time, General Eisenhower announced that he judged it necessary to concentrate more on his
flanks in the north and south. Behind this decision lay the not
unexpected, but now acute, danger that the Germans might be
ensconcing themselves for a fight to the bitter end, either in
Austria and Bavaria or in Norway. A winter campaign in Norway against a firmly entrenched enemy was considered "almost
impracticable", apart from the fact that with Scandinavia in
their hands the enemy's submarine warfare could continue for
some time. To guard against this, the Supreme Allied Comman-

The King's triumphant home-coming, 7 June 1945.

The Home Forces take over Akershus Castle from the Germans.

119

der revealed his intention to liberate Denmark first and then open the way to Norway through Sweden. Consequently, "operations to Berlin will have to take second place . . .".[1]

The prospect that had made Eisenhower effect such a momentous change in his plans had for a long time worried the Norwegian authorities, and diplomatic enquiries concerning the possibility of Swedish intervention had been made as early as 1 February that year. After indications that the British deprecated such plans, the matter had not been pursued beyond the diplomatic level, as moreover the initial Swedish reactions showed considerable reticence towards discussing the idea. The Swedes did not think it likely that the Germans would fight on in Norway unless provoked to do so. The Norwegian Government, however, could not share that optimism, and continued during April to press on the Allied Command the need to be prepared for large-scale operations in Norway.

The forces then at the disposal of the designated Allied Commander for the liberation of Norway consisted almost solely of Norwegian troops, since earmarked British troops had had to be sent to the Continent during the autumn and winter. Altogether there were now about 28,000 Norwegians in the armed services, of which the "police force" in Sweden made up one half and the brigade in Scotland numbered 4,000 men; the navy could muster 8,000 men and 52 ships, and the five squadrons of the Norwegian air force had altogether 2,600 men and about 80 planes of different kinds. In addition, the "Home Forces" of the Norwegian resistance movement at the time of the liberation numbered 40,000 men, most of them well trained, equipped, and armed. Against this, however, the German forces in Norway numbered altogether about 350—400,000 men.

Fortunately, as matters developed, it did not become necessary for the Allies to fight their way into Norway. In spite of considerable last minute confusion and uncertainty, the German commander in Norway acted in accordance with the general and complete surrender of all German forces. Shortly before the end, the Norwegian Government had cabled an authorisation to the leaders of the resistance to act on behalf of the Govern-

[1] Ehrman, *Grand Strategy*, Vol. VI (London, 1956), pp. 147—48.

ment in assuring the maintenance of order in the country, and to take steps for the establishment of a civil administration in accordance with previous agreements. During the night of 7-8 May, the Home Forces could then come out into the open. The official Allied armistice commission reached Oslo in the afternoon of 8 May, and from 9 May onwards Norwegian as well as recently provided British and American troops began to arrive in Norway.

On 13 May the first members of the Government could again set foot on Norwegian soil, accompanied by Crown Prince Olav as Supreme Commander of the Norwegian Armed Forces. And on 7 June, five years to the day after his departure for Britain and exile, King Haakon arrived in the Norwegian capital, where his welcome was an overwhelming demonstration of his popularity.

The post-war proceedings against enemy collaborators

THE FIRST PHASE

In the afternoon of 7 May 1945, it was reported over the radio that the German forces in Norway were capitulating. On the following day the Instrument of Surrender was signed. Norway was once more a free country. Over five years had passed since that April morning in 1940 when German forces at sea and in the air made their lightning attack on an unprepared country. On ceremonial occasions this period is frequently referred to as "the five long years". It had been a period full of humiliation and despair, of paralysing uncertainty, of fear and hope, of treason and failure, but also a period of national solidarity, of devotion and self-sacrifice.

The Norwegian Home Forces—numbering about 40,000— had remained under cover in order to be available in the event of an Allied invasion. Now, they emerged from their hide-outs and took over guard duties and the preservation of law and order. A couple of days later the Norwegian police forces, which had been trained in Sweden, began to cross the frontier.

During the first hours and days a number of dramatic events occurred among those who had previously held power. *Reichskommissar* Joseph Terboven and SS General Rediess blew themselves up in a bunker at Skaugum, the previous residence of the Crown Prince, which Terboven had taken over during the occupation. Some of the most desperate leaders of the Norwegian NS party—*Nasjonal Samling*—also took their own lives. Vidkun Quisling himself and a number of his "ministers" had gathered at Gimle, his magnificent residence just outside Oslo, surrounded by a company of the so-called Front Fighters (Norwegian volunteers for German service on the eastern front), and some of his Führer Guard. Quisling demanded to be treated as a head of state, but received the reply that he would be

The Home Forces emerge from their hide-outs on the afternoon of 7 May.

arrested by force if he failed to give himself up. In the morning of 9 May he arrived with his retinue at the police station in Oslo and was placed in custody.

At the same time the mass arrests of members of the NS party and other collaborators had begun according to plans which had been prepared in advance.

Not all members of the NS party were arrested—only those who had played a more prominent part or were suspected of specified crimes beyond the mere fact of party membership. According to the instructions, no arrest could be made except under a written warrant issued by a legally trained police official, but these instructions were not strictly adhered to everywhere in the hectic atmosphere prevailing at the time. On 1 July 1945, the number of prisoners was about 14,000. By the end of the year it had been reduced to less than 8,000, and continued to decline steadily.

Prisoners who were regarded as dangerous were placed in prison cells which became vacant when the former political prisoners of the Germans were released. Most prisoners, however, were placed in the concentration camps that the Germans and the Quisling authorities had established. The largest was Grini, near Oslo, which was renamed Ilebu after the war. Conditions in the prison camps were unsatisfactory at first because of their poor standard and on account of overcrowding. The food situation was also difficult in the beginning. However, these problems were overcome during the first few months. The prisoners' general state of health was good all the time, and no significant epidemics occurred.

Only in exceptional cases were attempts made to resist arrest, and in general the arrests were carried out in an orderly manner. During the occupation there had been much talk about the night of the long knives, when individual revenge would be taken. However, such scenes did not occur. The Government as well as the leaders of the Home Forces had forbidden the citizens to take the law into their own hands. In spite of the agitated atmosphere these orders were almost completely observed. One exception concerned the "German tarts", women who had kept company with German soldiers during the war. Their conduct was not criminal and accordingly they were not arrested, but in many places feelings against these women, who had outraged national sentiments during the war, were so strong that people took the matter into their own hands. A number of them had their hair cut off, and in some cases more severe treatment may have occurred. In order to avoid friction a large number of them were placed in protective detention, altogether over 1,000, but then many of these women were notorious prostitutes who were suspected of being carriers of venereal diseases. They were gradually released as the agitation subsided.

Public feeling ran high during the first months. The bitterness stored up during five years of oppression and frustrated fury burst forth and demanded satisfaction in some kind of reckoning with the offenders. Newspaper accounts of the crimes committed during the war, the abuse of power, informers, cruelty and torture—accounts which were not always well balanced—all contributed to inflame public sentiment.

By a kind of psychological process of identification, the general rage was vented on each individual collaborator, great or small, as if he had been responsible for it all. To mention that there might perhaps be excusing or mitigating circumstances was regarded by many as indicating a lack of national loyalty. Those who advocated moderation in the proceedings against the collaborators were said to be adopting a silky or velvety attitude. The unrelenting called themselves the ice front, a term which had been used during the occupation to describe the attitude of national resistance.

During the first period it was very difficult for the authorities to satisfy the popular demand for a quick, severe and thorough reckoning. The newspapers published angry letters about the many who went free, and about the appalling leniency in the treatment of arrested collaborators. In particular, the counsels for the defence engaged in the proceedings were strongly criticized, and accused of causing delay by invoking all kinds of formalities. Heavy criticism was voiced by the communists who, in 1940, at the time of the Soviet-German non-aggression pact, had been almost as pro-German as the NS party but afterwards, when Russia entered the war, had turned round completely and had been very active in the resistance movement. Resolutions poured in and protest meetings were arranged with thousands of participants demonstrating against the leniency and slow pace of the proceedings.

The violent feelings also led to some unfortunate episodes in the prison camps. The guards, consisting largely of Home Forces and police troops from Sweden, were mostly quite young men with no training or experience in the treatment of prisoners. Some of them had personal experience as inmates of prison camps and had acquired from the Germans and the NS police their ideas of how to handle prisoners. There were cases in which the guards—in their reaction to breaches of discipline, or even without any particular provocation—made use of irregular methods of punishment, such as strenuous drill and, in some cases, blows and kicks, or amused themselves by frightening the prisoners by firing over their heads or in other ways. Wherever it was possible in such cases to establish the facts of the offence and the identity of the offender, the authorities intervened by instituting criminal proceedings. In the propaganda against the sanctions imposed on the collaborators, these episodes have been magnified out of all proportions. Fantastic and terrifying descriptions have been given, with very little basis in fact. It could hardly have been expected that a settlement of such proportions, carried out with the assistance of thousands of young and untrained people—many of them with their nerves on edge after several years of active opposition to the occupation authorities—should have been accomplished without irregularities of any kind. However, the irregularities which did occur and which were mostly confined to the first days or weeks after the liberation, although regrettable, should be regarded as sporadic incidents. There was hardly any country where the liberation and the reaction against enemy collaborators took place in a calmer and more disciplined manner than in Norway.

Resentment against the collaborators found an outlet at first in a social boycott. Immediately after the liberation all members of the NS party were suspended from their public positions. Almost all private business firms adopted the same attitude. If an employer wished to keep a member of the NS party in his service, he usually had to choose between losing that man or losing the rest of his staff. After the members of the NS party, it was the turn of those who had not taken a sufficiently firm patriotic stand—the so-called striped or streaky ones. In many companies the workers went on strike in order to get rid of foremen or employees whom they considered to have been too submissive to the Germans or the NS. Nor was the boycott limited to business. In all kinds of clubs and associations similar purges took place. The dislike and contempt which had had to be kept under control during the war were now released and had free course. If warnings were given by people of moderation against turning all Quisling supporters into a class of untouchables, they were brushed aside as revealing a velvety attitude.

To Quisling supporters and their families this was a period of hardship. In a sense, those who had been interned and who were not exposed to daily censure suffered least. There were

Vidkun Quisling, photographed during his trial.

also some tragedies of suicide, one of them particularly moving.
A few days after the liberation it was reported in the press that
an NS prison director had killed his two children, his wife and
finally himself. When his father, an old teacher, heard what had
happened he and his wife took their own lives together.

THE QUISLING TRIAL

Some people had urged that Quisling ought to be brought
before a military court and shot after summary proceedings.
The authorities maintained that the normal judicial procedure
should be observed in this as in other cases.

On 20 August the preparations had been made and the main
hearing before the Criminal Court could begin. The trial lasted, with some interruptions, until 6 September. The shorthand court records are an important source of information on
this chapter of Norwegian history. Throughout the trial the
eyes of the world were focused on the provisional courtroom in
a large assembly hall in Oslo where the world's No. 1 quisling was

to be held responsible for his actions. The court was composed of three professional judges and four assessors who, together, were to decide the question of guilt as well as the penalty. The President of the Court was Erik Solem, one of the most distinguished judges in Norway. The functions of public prosecutor and counsel for the defence were also entrusted to eminent lawyers, Annæus Schjödt and Henrik Bergh respectively, both barristers to the Supreme Court of Norway. The well-known Swedish lawyer A. Hemming-Sjöberg, who attended the proceedings and afterwards published a book about the trial, wrote that "the principal parts in the great drama had thus been placed in the most qualified hands, and accordingly the proceedings were distinguished by objectivity, simplicity, concentration and dignity". He points out in particular that Quisling was treated like any other offender, and enjoyed all the rights of defence for which ample provision is made in Norwegian criminal procedure.

The charges concerned chiefly Quisling's activities during the war and the occupation of Norway: the proclamation of himself as head of government on 9 April 1940, his revocation of the order for mobilisation on the same day, his call for voluntary war efforts in support of Germany, his formation of a "government" on 1 February 1942, his complicity in the deportation of the Jews which cost several hundreds of them their lives, his responsibility for the execution of death sentences passed on Norwegian patriots, and a number of other counts. This alone would of course have been more than sufficient to qualify him for the law's highest penalty. However, there was another charge which from a moral point of view was particularly serious, and which, if proved, would therefore be an important factor in preventing the formation of a legend around the figure of Vidkun Quisling, namely that even before 9 April 1940 he had been an accomplice of the Germans, that he had received financial support from them, and assisted them in their planning of an attack on Norway. At the time the charges were being written, the evidence on this count was rather meagre, and as the trial approached the prosecuting authority was seriously considering whether it should be dropped. However, during the last weeks and days before the proceedings commenced, evidence began to pour in from the Norwegian representatives who were in Germany to study the German records. In particular, the Court based its conclusions on the diary of Alfred Rosenberg, on the testimony taken from German witnesses at Nuremberg for use in the Quisling trial, and on contemporary reports from German naval archives on Quisling's visit to Berlin in December 1939. The judgement quotes Rosenberg's diary for December 1939 which describes the visit made by Quisling and his assistant, Hagelin, and their conferences with Hitler and Grand Admiral Raeder. The final words of the notes on the visit were: "We shook hands and will probably not meet again until the action has been successfully completed, and the name of Norway's Ministerial President is Quisling."

One of the highlights of the trial was Quisling's great final speech in his own defence where—in a continuous statement of several hours—he reviewed his own life from childhood, his political efforts before the war, the failings of the old party leaders, his unselfish struggle to safeguard Norwegian interests during the occupation. On a pathetic note he concluded as follows:

"To me, politics is not a matter of party interests, professional job-seeking, or personal ambition and lust for power. It is a matter of self-sacrifice and practical action in the service of the historical development for the benefit of one's own country and to promote the realisation of God's Kingdom on earth which Christ came to establish.—If my activities have been treasonable—as they have been said to be—then I would pray to God that for the sake of Norway a large number of Norway's sons will become such traitors as I, but that they will not be thrown into jail."

There could be only one outcome of the trial. Quisling was found guilty on almost all counts, and by judgement of the Criminal Court on 10 September 1945 he was sentenced to death. Appeal was lodged with the Supreme Court of Norway which upheld the verdict by order of 13 October. A petition for reprieve submitted by Quisling's Russian-born wife was refused. In the early hours of 24 October 1945 his life ended before a firing squad.

Reference should be made to a legal point. There is no death penalty in Norway under the Penal Code of 1902. However, the death penalty had been maintained in the Military Penal Code of the same year. Quisling's treachery in the month of April 1940 came under the provisions of that Act, and might accordingly have carried the death penalty under the law as it stood at the time of the offence. Section 14 of that Act provided, however, that the death penalty could not be imposed or executed after the end of the war. It was pleaded for the defence that the war was now over and that, accordingly, the death penalty could not be imposed. The Supreme Court held that there was no need to discuss the definition of the term "end of the war" in § 14 of the Military Penal Code. Under a provisional enactment 3 October 1941 of the Norwegian Government in London, and confirmed by the Storting after the liberation, it had been provided that—notwithstanding the provision of § 14 of the Military Penal Code—the death sentence could be imposed and executed after the end of the war. The Court discussed whether the application of the 1941 enactment to Quisling's conduct would be contrary to § 97 of the Constitution, which provides that no law shall have retroactive effect. The Court came to the conclusion that this was not so. Any person who—before the provisional enactment—was guilty of a crime which could entail the death penalty, might have some *prospect* of avoiding the death penalty, i.e. if he could not be sentenced and executed before the end of the war, but in the opinion of the Supreme Court the offender had no *protected right* to such relief.

LEGISLATIVE POWERS OF THE NORWEGIAN GOVERNMENT IN EXILE

Even before the Quisling case, certain points of principle had begun to come up for consideration by the courts in connection with other groups of collaborators. On 9 August 1945, a member of the NS police who had been guilty of outrageous acts of torture had been sentenced to death by the Supreme Court (the Haaland Case). A few weeks later the first sentences were passed on Norwegians who had taken part as volunteers on the German side during the war, and also on ordinary members of the NS party.

The first point of principle to be dealt with by the courts was whether the Norwegian Government in exile in London had powers to legislate. It was pleaded by the defence that the Government had no legislative authority—or at least no such authority with effect in the occupied territory—and that the enactments it had passed, e.g. for the extended use of capital punishment and for special rules of procedure in cases of collaboration, were therefore invalid. This objection was unanimously rejected by the Supreme Court. The Court considered it hardly doubtful that the situation which arose from the German assault on 9 April 1940 was such as to invest the executive power, as the only remaining free agency of government, with "the right to take the measures necessitated by the war and the conditions resulting therefrom for the purpose of upholding the nation's freedom and independence, and in general of protecting or safeguarding Norwegian interests, including the prepararation of the judicial proceedings which would have to take place once the war had ended". In the premises for its conclusion the Court also referred to the powers vested in the Government by the Storting at its session at Elverum in the evening of 9 April 1940.

It has been argued that such legislative powers for the exiled Government are contrary to the provision of the Land War Rules of the Hague Convention under which the legislative authority in the occupied territory passes to the occupying power. This is a mistaken view. The occupant has such legislative power as is required to maintain law and order, and to prevent attacks on his interests; he also possesses a limited right to requisition goods and services from the inhabitants. But he has no right to require the citizens to commit treason. Accordingly, if the punishment for treason is made more severe, or if special provisions are made to facilitate the prosecution of traitors, there is no conflict between the so-called obedience due to the occupant, and the loyalty due to the lawful authorities. It might be discussed what the position would be if the

Government in exile had required the citizens of occupied territory—under threat of punishment—to engage in active resistance to the occupying power. However, there was no question of any such requirement.

Related to the question of the Government's legislative power is the significance of the fact that the Government had been unable to promulgate its enactments in the ordinary way in the occupied territory. It was pleaded by the defence that new provisions which increased the penalty for certain offences could not be applicable already from the moment the provisions were adopted, but were applicable only to offences committed after the provisions had been promulgated in Norway. This objection too was rejected. Even before the war it had been held by the Norwegian courts that the validity of a new law did not depend on whether it had been promulgated. The prohibition in § 97 of the Constitution against giving a law retroactive effect means only that the new law does not apply to acts committed previously. It does not prevent a new law from having effect on future acts, even if they are committed before the offender has had an opportunity to acquaint himself with the new law. In any case, most of the enactments had been promulgated by such means as were available in the circumstances, i.e. by having them published in the Norwegian Gazette in London, by radio broadcasts, by dropping leaflets, etc. In the opinion of the Supreme Court this should in any case have been sufficient.

The Enactment of 15 December 1944 relating to Collaboration with the Enemy was in a special position in that it had not been promulgated at all, perhaps because it was feared at the time that it might lead to reprisals against the population. A minority of the Court took the view that an enactment which had actually been kept secret could not be regarded as valid law in relation to people who were not aware of it. The majority, however, came to the opposite result, holding that this would not lead to any injustice since any person who committed treason against his country under the prevailing circumstances had every reason to expect new penal provisions to become applicable to such conduct.

The entire system of the post-war criminal proceedings against enemy collaborators rests on two sections of the Penal Code of 1902. Section 86 concerns those who "unlawfully grant assistance to the enemy by word or deed", and section 98 concerns those who "cause or contribute to any change, by unlawful means, in the Constitution of the Kingdom".

Section 86 relating to assistance to the enemy was the most important provision in the judicial proceedings. This provision has later been modified by an Act of 15 December 1950, which gave it a more detailed formulation, though without altering its essential content.

Because of its general formulation this provision has a very wide range of application. It applies equally whether the assistance is on a large or small scale, whether it is direct or indirect, whether it is motivated by selfish or idealistic reasons. Accordingly, the provision covers all kinds of unlawful assistance, from the most serious and outrageous acts of treason, which require the law's severest penalty, to quite trivial cases of assistance due to political foolishness or weakness.

Section 86 was applied to Quisling himself, besides many other sections of the Civil and Military Penal Codes; it was used against the Quisling ministers and other leading collaborators, against the employees of the NS police, spies, agents and informers, contractors and workers who had entered enemy service, etc.

There has been much discussion of whether ordinary members of the NS party come under this provision. It is clear enough that the NS as such supported the enemy. And since any membership constituted support of the activities of the party as a whole, it is logically incontestable that membership of the party gave indirect support to the enemy. However, law is not the same as logic. One may well ask: Is not such indirect assistance too insignificant to warrant the application of so serious a penal provision? The first time this question came up for decision in the Supreme Court, dissenting opinions were expressed. The majority, consisting of seven judges, held that § 86 was applicable; the minority, four judges, felt that the individual member's adherence to the party was so remotely and indirectly connected with the persistent criminal activities of the party leaders, that it should not be deemed to constitute assistance to the enemy. In subsequent cases the majority view was applied without the question having been reopened.

In their attemps to discredit the judicial proceedings, members of the NS party have made the doubt on this point one of their major arguments. The range of penalties provided in § 86 is frequently invoked against the view taken by the Supreme Court: from a minimum of three years imprisonment to a maximum imprisonment for life. Surely nobody would think of passing sentence of three years imprisonment on a passive member of the NS party. This, it is held, shows that the provision is not intended for such cases. But in support of the Supreme Court's decision it is argued that one cannot read each provision of a law in isolation. The range of punishment in § 86 is modified by a general rule in § 58 of the Penal Code which provides that in cases where several persons have co-operated for a criminal purpose, the punishment may be reduced to less than the normal minimum and to a milder kind, e.g. in regard to the offenders whose participation "has been of slight importance compared to that of the others". The conduct of ordinary members of the NS party was undoubtedly a matter of "slight importance" compared with the crimes of the leaders. Under § 58 it was therefore possible, even without the Collaboration Enactment, to impose a fine, with or without the loss of civil rights.

However, the question of punishment for membership does not depend entirely on an interpretation of § 86 of the Penal Code. As early as January 1942 the Government in London had issued an enactment directed explicitly against those who kept up their membership of the NS. The validity of this enactment has been unanimously accepted by the Supreme Court. Accordingly, the interpretation of § 86 has practical bearing only on the small number of people who had left the party before January 1942, most of whom have not been prosecuted. Besides, the Supreme Court unanimously held that membership of the NS could come under § 98 of the Penal Code as constituting participation in an attempt unlawfully to change the Constitution.

The Penal Code emphasizes that only cases of *unlawful* assistance to the enemy come under its provisions. In the Collaboration Enactment the same limitation is expressed in the requirement that an act, in order to constitute an offence, must be *improper*. If a person has knowingly assisted the enemy, his action is still not an offence unless it was improper, i.e. unless it violated the general standard of national conduct. This is a limitation which is particularly important under conditions of occupation.

To put it simply, the population and public officials are faced with a choice of two alternatives during a state of occupation: either a policy of chaos, by refusing any kind of voluntary co-operation with the occupying power and accepting the consequent suffering and want; or a policy of co-operation in business and administration to such extent as is necessary to ensure endurable and orderly conditions, even if this also benefits the enemy in some measure. In Norway the latter alternative was already adopted during the period of the Administrative Council in 1940, and this was supported by the population. Although the hostile attitude to the occupying power was intensified later, it never became the prevailing view that all economic connection with the Germans should cease and that all public employees should retire.

Such a policy places the individual in a difficult position. And afterwards it becomes even more difficult to draw the line between permissible and improper co-operation at any time. This has proved particularly hard in matters of economic co-operation with the occupying power. The extreme cases are clear enough. There was a general agreement, on the one hand, that anybody who had not voluntarily engaged in activities for the benefit of the enemy, but had only complied with a requisition which was lawful under international law, could not be punished. On the other hand, it was equally clear that anybody who had voluntarily engaged in activities of military importance for the Germans, activities which had not served Norwegian interests at the same time, was considered to have acted improperly and hence to have committed an offence. All other cases, however, had to be decided on their specific merits, with regard to such factors as the relative military importance of the work performed, its bearing on Norwegian interests, the extent of the work, the motives of the businessman and the interest he had shown in getting the contract, etc.

In principle, ordinary workers on German construction projects could also be sentenced under the rules against enemy collaboration. Taking the view that it was impossible in practice to deal with everybody whose conduct might be criticized, the Collaboration Enactment provided an opportunity to waive punishment in respect of those who had worked in a purely subordinate capacity. The Chief Public Prosecutor laid down the general rule that punishment should normally be inflicted only on those who had left regular and well paid Norwegian work in order to perform work of direct military importance to the Germans. Even so, the prosecution of collaborators of this kind was rather ineffective, because it exceeded the capacity of the authorities to investigate all the tens of thousands who had taken work on German construction projects, with a view to ascertaining whether there had been such aggravating circumstances.

It can hardly be denied that in practice, owing to technical difficulties, the reaction against enemy collaborators had a somewhat lopsided effect. Members of the NS were registered and could thus be clearly distinguished. It proved more difficult to define other forms of unpatriotic conduct.

The difficulty of defining the term "improper conduct" was clearly reflected in the cases against the three "ministers" appointed by *Reichskommissar* Terboven who had not been members of the NS. The circumstances were somewhat different in each case, but common to them all was that they had accepted the appointment in order to protect Norwegian interests, not with the intention of supporting the Germans or the NS party; that they had conducted their ministries in an excellent way and had resisted attempts at nazification; and that they had resigned when Quisling formed his "government" on 1 February 1942. A minority of the Supreme Court held that they had such good reasons for their decision that their conduct could not be considered unlawful. The majority, however, held that their conduct had been unlawful but some of these judges found their mistake so excusable as to warrant acquittal on that ground. In conclusion they were all acquitted. One of them, who had held high public office since before the war, was declared entitled to retain that position. This result has been the subject of much discussion.

As pointed out above, every kind of assistance to the enemy comes under the law, provided it was improper. On the other hand the law does not apply to all kinds of *unpatriotic conduct*. For this reason, the "German tarts" were not prosecuted. The arrests made during the early stages were in the nature of police measures intended to maintain law and order during a critical period. Nor did the law apply to other private dealings with the Germans, even though they might be very degrading from a national point of view. On the other hand, such conduct might be taken into account in determining whether a public employee had proved himself unworthy of his position. Nor was any sentence passed on clergymen and teachers who, while not being members of the NS, failed in their resistance to the "New Order", but they were deprived of their public positions by court order, unless special circumstances could be pleaded in excuse.

WAS NORWAY AT WAR?

Assistance to the enemy could not be considered as constituting an offence, unless Norway was at war with Germany during the occupation. At first after the liberation the existence of a state of war during the occupation was considered so self-evident that the question was not even raised by the defence. Later on the situation changed. It is now generally argued by former NS members and others affected by the judicial proceedings, that the war came to an end at the time of the capitulation in northern Norway in June 1940. This view is based, in particular, on the German text of the Capitulation Agreement of 10 June, which contains a clause stating that "All the Norwegian armed forces will lay down their arms and undertake not to resort to arms against the German Reich or its allies as long as the present war lasts." This Agreement between representatives of the two High Commands, which was intended to arrange practical matters in connection with the capitulation, has been recalled from oblivion and proclaimed as an act of the highest importance: it is even said that the authorities have tried to keep it secret.

Such an interpretation is clearly untenable, and it was unanimously rejected by the Supreme Court in a judgment of 6 March 1948, where the question was taken up for thorough discussion. The Capitulation Agreement was a military agreement relating to the surrender of the remaining Norwegian forces in northern Norway, the only place where fighting was still going on; it was no political agreement about the relations between the states of Germany and Norway. This is also shown in the preamble to the Agreement: "In view of the courage shown by the 6th Division, the following honourable terms are granted for its surrender." Under the Norwegian Constitution, matters of war and peace are decided by the King in Council, not by the military high commands. We know from German as well as from Norwegian sources that the limited scope of the Capitulation Agreement was made quite clear to the Germans by the Norwegian negotiators. To interpret the Capitulation Agreement as having any bearing on the question of whether the state of war continued would be in direct conflict with the other facts of the situation. In a proclamation of 7 June, which was broadcast by Tromsö Radio on 9 June, the King and the Government made it clear that although the fighting in Norway had to be discontinued, it would continue beyond the nation's borders. The military forces were small at first, but were gradually increased although they never attained any considerable numerical strength. As early as the summer and autumn of 1940, the Government issued a number of provisional enactments which were made valid "during the present state of war" or "as long as Norway is at war" – this latter term being already used in an enactment of 12 July concerning the registration of Norwegian nationals abroad. On the German side the attitude alternated as the situation required: at times the Germans declared that a state of war existed between the two countries; at times they insisted that the German forces had come

138

to protect Norway against an Allied invasion. A clear indication of the state of war was the fact that the Germans, in the autumn of 1943, arrested the Norwegian officers and sent them as prisoners of war to Germany.

On balance, there can be no reasonable doubt about the existence of a state of war, under international law as well as under Norwegian criminal law. It cannot be denied, however, that in the first months there was considerable uncertainty among the population. Thus, in the summer of 1940, it was apparently no unusual view that the war between Norway and Germany actually ended with the capitulation in Norway, and that Norwegians who continued the war abroad were to be regarded as volunteers whose activities did not commit the state of Norway. At the time, a distinguished lawyer in Trondheim wrote a newspaper article to that effect, which has since been frequently invoked. Some confusion was presumably felt as regards the legal situation, particularly no doubt among members of the NS. In criminal law, however, this is no exculpating circumstance. According to general principles of criminal law it is sufficient that the accused has been aware of the relevant factual circumstances—in this case that the nation had taken up arms against the German assault, that peace had not been concluded, and that the King and the Government continued the struggle outside the nation's borders. It makes no difference whether the accused was aware of the precise limitation of the legal concept of "war"

ATTACKS ON THE CONSTITUTION

In addition to § 86, the other main provision on which the judicial proceedings were based is § 98 of the Penal Code, relating to attacks on the Constitution. Whereas § 86 applied to one aspect of the activities of Quisling and his supporters, namely that they made common cause with the enemy in the struggle against the lawful Government and its allies, § 98 applied to another aspect of those activities, namely that the NS party—contrary to the will of the majority of the population and supported by German bayonets—sought to alter the Constitution and replace the principle of democracy by the autocracy of the Führer state. The Supreme Court declared that this provision—like § 86— applied also to ordinary members of the NS. In practice however, § 98 was used to a lesser extent; and only against the more prominent leaders of the party. Perhaps this was a mistake from a psychological point of view. The "New Order" was at the very centre of the party's activities, and no doubt contributed just as much as the actual co-operation with the enemy to create the violent reaction against the party. More widespread use of this provision would have eliminated many of the objections that were raised by the convicted collaborators. For one thing, the application of § 98 is not based on the assumption that a state of war existed. And many of the convicted collaborators were prepared to admit that they were guilty of rebellion, but reacted violently against a sentence for treason.

THE COLLABORATION ENACTMENT

The major offenders were tried directly under the provisions of the Penal Code of 1902. Minor offenders such as ordinary NS members and small profiteers were tried under the provisions of the so-called Collaboration Enactment of 15 December 1944, which was subsequently superseded by an Act of February 1947 containing roughly the same provisions. The Collaboration Enactment has played such a large part in the debate on the judicial proceedings that it deserves description in some detail:

The forerunner of the Collaboration Enactment was the already mentioned Enactment of January 1942, which was directed against those who kept up their membership in the NS party or in other organizations which afforded assistance to the enemy. This Enactment was based on the assumption—which was also reflected in its wording—that membership in the NS constituted the punishable offence of assistance to the enemy, provided the subjective conditions of guilt were satisfied, and it was presumed that this would nearly always be the case. The

Enactment involved a certain extension of the criminal liability by making such membership an offence even if the member was unaware that he was assisting the enemy by virtue of his membership. The main significance of the Enactment, however, was not this extension of the criminal liability, but that it unequivocally expressed the attitude of the law to the NS party, and that it provided for the forfeiture of public confidence and the imposition of fines, in addition to the penalties provided in the Penal Code itself. The loss of public confidence, which could be inflicted for life, or for a specified number of years, included not only political rights—the right to vote, the right to serve with the armed forces, and the right to hold public office —but also the right to exercise certain trades and professions (e.g. that of lawyer, medical practitioner, merchant or master craftsman), and the right to act as an officer of any business company or association. In a broadcast announcing the Enactment, Terje Wold, then Minister of Justice, later Chief Justice of the Norwegian Supreme Court, put it this way: "One may say that a person who is sentenced to deprivation of public confidence, is expelled—in an economic, social and political sense—from the community to which he has proved himself unworthy to belong."

The Collaboration Enactment of 1944, which superseded the Enactment of 1942, represented on the whole a milder approach. It had been drafted in Norway by a committee appointed by the leaders of the resistance movement, and was given its final form by the Government in London. The ideas expressed in the drafting of the Enactment were these: the ordinary provisions concerning treason and attacks on the Constitution are as such also applicable to ordinary members of the NS and others who have given the Germans relatively insignificant assistance, for instance an ordinary worker on German construction projects. However, the penalties provided in the Penal Code have not been stipulated with a view to conditions during a lengthy occupation. Over a period of five years of occupation there are many who have violated the provisions, but not so seriously as to make it justifiable or feasible to call them all to account under the provisions of the Penal Code. In order to enable the courts freely to choose the appropriate sanction in each particular case, the Enactment provided for the imposition of fines or short-term prison sentences on minor offenders. Further, it provided for limited deprivation of civil rights instead of the complete loss of public confidence under the Enactment of 1942, besides providing a possibility of granting complete exemption from punishment in certain cases, as when the offence had been committed under duress or by a person below 18 years of age, or in cases where a member of the NS party had afterwards rendered patriotic service to the resistance movement.

Because of the way in which it was formulated, the Enactment has given rise to much misunderstanding. Instead of containing provisions authorizing a reduction in the penalty for certain categories of offenders, the Enactment was given the form of separate penal provisions with corresponding degrees of punishment in respect of those who after 8 April 1940 had been members of the NS, had engaged or participated in improper business activities for the enemy, or had otherwise violated the provisions concerning treason or rebellion. Technically, therefore, the Enactment gives the appearance of a Penal Act relating to offences which have already been committed, and this has led to the allegation that the judicial proceedings were based on an enactment in violation of the Constitutional prohibition against making laws retroactive. The reality of the matter is that the Enactment – according to the legal view on which it is based, and which has been accepted by the courts – applies to acts that were criminal under the previous provisions, and authorizes milder sentences than they do.

In some respects, however, the provisions of the Collaboration Enactment were more stringent than the previous ones, or one could at least suspect that this was so. This applied to the rules relating to the confiscation of unlawful gain, the joint economic responsibility of the offender's spouse, the enforcement of economic liability, and a few others. Since, under Norwegian constitutional law, the courts have the right and obligation to void unconstitutional laws, they were obliged in each particular case to decide whether the new provisions conflicted with the prohibition in § 97 of the Constitution against retroactive legislation. However, it is hardly necessary to go into detail on this point, since most of the severer rules of the Collaboration Enactment were either already abolished in the autumn of 1945, or proved to be of little or no practical consequence. However, one point of principle should be noted, namely the joint economic liability imposed on the members of the NS.

The Collaboration Enactment provided that those who had been guilty of membership in the NS "are jointly and severally liable for the damage which that organization has caused by its complicity in the unlawful administration of the country, or by other unlawful acts." The authors of the Enactment assumed that such liability existed in any case under the law of torts, according to the general rule that if several people have acted together in causing damage, they are jointly liable for the payment of compensation. It is very doubtful whether this view is correct. The present writer has expressed the opinion that the previous principles of liability for torts could not be stretched so far. The decision of the Supreme Court was awaited with great interest. In a judgement of 8 September 1945 the Supreme Court—voting eight to three—accepted the view on which the Collaboration Enactment was based and, accordingly, the question whether the provision was unconstitutional as having retroactive effect did not arise.

Actually, however, this joint liability did not assume such significance as might have been expected. According to the original wording of the Collaboration Enactment, the liability was to be enforced to the full extent of the offender's property. And as the total damage caused by the misuse of public funds, unlawful imprisonments and confiscations, etc., amounted to several hundred million kroner, i. e. much more than the total assets of all NS members in the whole country, the actual result would have been—as was pointed out at the time—that every single member of the NS party would have gone bankrupt. It would for instance have meant that all NS farmers would have had to leave their farms. The social consequences of such a rule would evidently have been extremely serious. However, only a few months after the liberation the rule was modified by a new enactment of 3 August, 1945 which provided that the liability should be assessed in each particular case at an amount which the court considered to be reasonable having regard to the degree of guilt and the economic circumstances of the offender. As a result, this liability provision did not prove to be of much consequence, except perhaps in the case of wealthy offenders. In fact, the same elements – the gravity of the crime and the offender's economic circumstances – were taken into consideration for the purpose both of stipulating the fine and of stipulating the amount of damages; and, under Norwegian law, there is no limit to the fine which may be imposed. For the courts, the essential point was to arrive at an over-all amount which was reasonable in relation to the offence. How the amount was divided between the fine and the compensation was a subordinate matter.

It can hardly be denied that the Collaboration Enactment bears somewhat too strong an impression of the conditions under which it was drafted, in strict secrecy and under the greatest personal risk by people at the head of the resistance movement, people who, by the very circumstances under which they lived, inevitably took a severe view of those who betrayed the national unity. Subsequent amendments modified this impression, but did not entirely remove it. It would presumably have been an advantage if, instead of the Collaboration Enactment, a special provision had simply been issued authorizing the courts to reduce the ordinary penalty for acts of treason committed during the occupation. It would not have made much practical difference in the proceedings, since the necessary penal provisions already existed. But many points of doubt would have been avoided which arose from the Enactment and which have been exploited to the extreme in the attempts to discredit the judicial proceedings against the collaborators.

A QUANTITATIVE SURVEY OF
THE PROCEEDINGS

On account of the comprehensive formulation of the penal provisions which came into operation, the judicial proceedings assumed vast proportions. Over 90,000 cases were investigated by the police. About 46,000 persons were found guilty. 18,000 of these were sentenced to imprisonment, sometimes also to the payment of a fine and the loss of civil rights, while 28,000 were only fined and/or deprived of civil rights. In another 5,000 cases the prosecuting authority considered the offender guilty, but made no charge because of the insignificance of the offence or the existence of particularly mitigating circumstances.

Of the 18,000 prison sentences about 4,500 were for more than three years, and about 600 for more than eight years. It should be noted that these are the terms stipulated in the sentence, not the time actually served. According to the general rule of the Prison Act, a prisoner is released after having served two thirds of his term if his conduct has been satisfactory. Under an Act adopted in the summer of 1948, the period of imprisonment for collaborators was reduced, with certain exceptions, to one-half of the term under the sentence. A collaborator who had been arrested immediately after the liberation and sentenced to eight years imprisonment or hard labour had thus normally finished serving his sentence by the summer of 1949. The principle of halving the period of imprisonment did not apply to sentences of more than eight years, since it was assumed that some of these prisoners were dangerous people who should be dealt with individually. However, under a system of reprieve, collaborators serving sentences of more than eight years were also released after having served half their term, and gradually after an even shorter period. For prisoners sentenced to twenty years, the average time served was about six and a half years. Altogether there were 80 persons who had either been sentenced to life imprisonment or whose death sentence had been commuted to imprisonment for life. For this group the average time served was about nine years, which is considerably less than the average time for criminals in general who are sentenced to life

145

imprisonment. The last prisoners were released in November 1957, after having served about twelve and a half years of their sentence.

Three years after the liberation the number of prisoners was still almost 4,000. After another three years the figure had fallen to about 150. Thus, only a relatively small number of offenders served really long terms of imprisonment.

To the police and courts the proceedings meant a very heavy strain. Before the war the annual number of persons convicted of crimes in Norway—not misdemeanours—was about 4,000. Now, collaboration cases many times more numerous had to be dealt with in addition to the ordinary criminal cases and the many extraordinary police functions involved in the liberation. Moreover, the police had to be completely reorganized, since many of the officials who had served with the prosecuting authority and the police during the war were removed from their positions. A large number of new and inexperienced people had to take over.

It had been assumed in advance that the proceedings would take about one year. This calculation proved to be entirely wrong, partly because the number of cases was much larger than anticipated, partly because it took much longer to deal with each case than had been expected. It had been assumed that once the points of basic principle had been decided, and certain standards of sentencing developed, the rest of the cases could be dealt with "by conveyor belt methods". It was found, however, that practically every single case had its peculiarities —whether of a mitigating or aggravating kind—and the judges stuck to the old doctrine that each case should be judged on its own merits, and that any doubt should benefit the accused. Nor can one doubt that many of the accused had an interest in prolonging the proceedings, considering that the passage of time, which heals all wounds, would also lead to a milder result in their case. After one year, less than one third of the cases had been finally dealt with. One year later, about three quarters of the cases had been concluded. A few cases even took much longer, for special reasons. In particular, the cases involving improper business activities for the enemy proved to be complicated.

In order to speed up the proceedings, the Enactment relating to procedure in cases of collaboration provided a possibility of settling the case without bringing it to court, by giving the offender the choice of accepting a penalty stipulated by the prosecuting authority. This is a system which is widely used also in ordinary criminal procedure to settle trifling cases. It was now provided that the offender could be given this choice of accepting a penalty in all cases where the penalty was only a fine and/or the loss of civil rights. Most of the charges against ordinary members of the Nazi Party were settled in this manner. Later the system was extended to include penalties of imprisonment for up to one year. This was done mainly in order to simplify the procedure for those who had already been held in custody for a period of time approximately equivalent to the sentence which might be expected.

THE DEATH SENTENCE

One of the aspects of the settlement with the enemy collaborators which had the greatest emotional impact was the use of capital punishment. Since 1876 there had been no executions in Norway, and for non-military cases the death penalty was formally abolished by the Penal Code of 1902, though it was maintained in the Military Penal Code. By enactments of the Norwegian Government in London during the occupation, capital punishment was introduced for acts of civilian treason as well. The reason given was that at the time when the Penal Code of 1902 was written, one could hardly realize how outrageous a case of treason could be and what consequences it could have for the nation as a whole. Nowadays civilian treason may be just as disastrous as military treason and it was therefore considered pointless to distinguish between them. At the same time the previous provision of the Military Penal Code stipulating that the death penalty could not be imposed or executed after the end of the war, was repealed. The possibility of applying the death penalty to war crimes, e.g. German acts of torture and the killing of hostages, was also greatly extended. After the liberation these enactments relating to capital punishment were submitted to the Storting, and approved against only a few votes.

Now, to what extent did the courts make use of their right to impose the death sentence?

Altogether, 45 final death sentences were passed, 30 on Norwegian collaborators, 15 on German war criminals. Of these, 37 have been executed—25 of the Norwegians and 12 of the Germans.

Only three political leaders were given death sentences, namely Quisling himself and two of his "ministers". The other "ministers" received prison sentences, either for life or for a limited period.

All the others who were sentenced to death had been guilty of appalling acts of torture, or of killing prisoners, or of causing the death of their countrymen by acting as informers under aggravating circumstances. The largest group of death sentences resulted from the trials of the notorius "Rinnan gang". Ten of the members were sentenced to death, eleven to hard labour for life, and many others to long terms of imprisonment. But then the crimes committed by the gang were no minor affair: they caused over one thousand active participants in the Norwegian resistance movement to be exposed and arrested; almost a hundred lost their lives, and several hundred were subjected to vicious and systematic torture. The leader of the gang, Henry Rinnan, was personally convicted of thirteen murders.

The number of death sentences and executions was far smaller than most people had expected at the time of the liberation. Influenced by the war and its disregard of human life, the general opinion at first was that the courts were too restrained in passing sentence of death. Gradually, however, opposition to capital punishment increased. Whereas, in 1945, only six members of the Storting voted against the death sentence, a proposal in 1948 to discontinue the use of capital punishment was rejected in the Lower House of the Storting by only 62 to 43 votes. Gradually, as the wartime conditions receded into the past, the prosecuting authority and the courts

The President of the Criminal Court pronounces the sentence on Quisling.

also became less inclined to demand and impose the death sentence. At the same time, the right of reprieve was increasingly exercised. The last execution took place in the autumn of 1948.

THE PRINCIPLES OF SENTENCING

Among all the thousands of cases involved in the post-war settlement, no two are exactly alike. However, by selecting certain typical groups as examples it may be possible to give an idea of the standards applied in determining the penalties. It may be noted that in Norway the penalty as such may be brought in appeal before the Supreme Court, by the convicted party as well as by the prosecuting authority, and this right was indeed extensively used in the proceedings against the collaborators. Thus, it was the Supreme Court which eventually drew up the general principles for the choice of punishment.

Generally speaking, the sentences tended to become less severe as time went by. To some extent, this may have a rational justification. Offenders whose cases were not dealt with until two, three or four years after the liberation, had suffered a severe strain during the long period of waiting, and this might reasonably be taken into account in stipulating the punishment.

In certain respects there may also have been a reappraisal of circumstances as more information about war-time events was obtained, and a more differentiated picture emerged. Mainly, however, it was probably a psychological phenomenon of fatigue which came into play as the mass punishments continued and the indignation at the war-time events subsided.

A fairly uniform group consists of the so-called Front Fighters, i.e. Norwegian volunteers for German service on the eastern front. For this group the first sentences were for periods of four to eight years according to the man's age and circumstances and duration of service. Later, a period of three to four years was the usual sentence for adult Front Fighters, while the younger ones were on the whole given considerably milder punishment. The first sentences have subsequently been reduced to this level by the granting of pardons. For officers of senior rank, the sentences were far more severe in some cases.

In connection with the Front Fighters, some mention should be made of the women who had served in the German Red Cross. This is a matter which has been discussed a great deal. It was argued that the purpose of the Red Cross is to tend both friend and foe, and that such service was therefore humanitarian rather than warlike. This view was not accepted by the courts. The first Red Cross nurse to be placed on trial was sentenced to fully three years imprisonment, on the view that a member of the medical corps is no less important to the war effort than an ordinary soldier, and that a female nurse should be judged by the same standard. However, this sentence caused a reaction, and subsequent sentences were usually for periods of about one year and sometimes considerably less. In some cases the sentence was suspended, either by the court or by Royal Pardon.

Numerically, the largest group of offenders were the members of the NS party. Naturally, their sentences varied a great deal according to the position and activities of each member. Ordinary members who had not committed specific acts of treason received no prison sentence, but had to pay a fine and lost their voting rights for ten years. Persons who did not own any property were usually ordered to pay a fine of 500 or 1,000 kroner, while heavy fines were imposed on those having capital resources. A few examples may illustrate this:

A businessman in his sixties, owning property worth kroner 350,000, was ordered to pay a fine of kroner 40,000 and a compensation of kroner 160,000, making a total of kroner 200,000. In addition to his membership of the NS he had carried out certain propaganda activities and had paid contributions to the Norwegian Legion—a Norwegian contingent which took part with the German forces on the eastern front. A purely passive member owning kroner 700,000 was ordered to pay a fine and compensation totalling kroner 300,000. The view was that the unpatriotic conduct of the rich man too should lead to a noticeable reduction in his financial position. On the other hand, the courts followed the principle that the punishment should not make it impossible for the offender to continue his business, a principle which has been of particular importance to the farmers who had been members of the NS.

With regard to the so-called "economic collaborators"—the profiteers—the courts concentrated on the economic sanction. Naturally, the profits derived from their unlawful activities were confiscated and in addition they were deprived of their civil rights and ordered to pay fines in varying amounts. In more serious cases, prison sentences were also imposed, some of them for several years. A very well-known case concerned a businessman whose actual offence had not been very serious, but who had a special responsibility because of his prominent position in business circles. He was sentenced to imprisonment for one year, and to pay a fine of 2 million kroner, the highest fine ever imposed in the history of this country.

There has been a great deal of discussion about the sentences involving the loss of civil rights. As mentioned above, the type of punishment described as "loss of public confidence" was introduced by the Enactment of January 1942, relating to punishment for membership in the NS party. It was further developed by the Collaboration Enactment of 1944, which provided that any person who was sentenced to the loss of public confidence, thereby also lost the right to own or hold real estate. However, the courts disliked a form of punishment which—to quote the Supreme Court—would cause an offender who had served his term of imprisonment to be debarred from acquiring a small farm or beginning as a cultivator of new land, and thus to be deprived of an opportunity to earn a position in the community which might otherwise be open to him. As a matter of fact, only a limited loss of civil rights was inflicted; minor offenders lost their voting rights and the rights to serve in the armed forces; in more severe cases they were also deprived of the right to take employment in public service and to exercise certain professional or business rights for a certain period of time such as the right to practice as a lawyer or contractor. Public opinion at first demanded that for instance doctors and dentists who were convicted of collaboration should be sentenced to lose their right to practice, but the courts did not give in to this demand. Only in a few special cases where the offences were related to the actual exercise of the profession did the courts deprive the offender of his right to practice.

A far stricter attitude was taken towards civil servants and other public officials. In their case even passive membership in the NS led to dismissal from their positions, unless there were very special extenuating circumstances, for example that the official, protected by his membership, had granted assistance to the underground movement. The courts here took the view that a higher degree of loyalty should be demanded of public servants than of other citizens. This rule may often have seemed harsh, particularly in respect of employees in subordinate positions who had joined the party under pressure from above. Generally, the courts have not denied such offenders the right to future employment in government service. The possibility then remained for the offender to return to such service, perhaps in a more modest and less conspicuous position than before.

As indicated above, a public official could be sentenced to the loss of his position, even without being guilty of any criminal offence, if his conduct had been so unpatriotic as to make him unworthy to continue in his position. Some officials were given only a disciplinary punishment, e.g. suspension of service for one year without pay, and some were allowed to resign of their own accord.

THE CASE OF KNUT HAMSUN

One of the most disputed cases during the proceedings was the trial of the famous author and Nobel Prize winner Knut Hamsun. His fate continues to concern people to this day. In 1978, the well-known Danish author, Thorkild Hansen, published his book "The Hamsun Trial" which gave new life to the debate. In Thorkild Hansen's opinion Hamsun was unfairly and inconsiderately treated by the Norwegian legal authorities. He portrays Hamsun as a genius who fell victim to vindictiveness and pettiness on the part of the authorities. Similar views have been expressed by several Norwegian writers.

What was the prosecution's case against Hamsun? He had written a number of articles during the war which, objectively speaking, constituted flagrant treason. Already during the campaign in Norway in the spring of 1940, he sided with the Germans, scorning the Cabinet which had sought refuge in the interior of the country, and appealing to Norwegian soldiers to throw down their guns and go home. Furthermore, throughout the war Hamsun supported Quisling and his party "Nasjonal Samling"; he participated in the propaganda campaign to enlist Norwegian military support of Germany, and he encouraged Norwegian seamen in Allied trades to escape and return to Norway. In an article celebrating the tenth anniversary of the NS party he wrote: "I think things are going very well now, with the submarines working night and day." The NS as well as the Germans naturally exploited the famous name of Hamsun to the utmost in their propaganda. But the majority of the Norwegian people was profoundly angered and disappointed by his behaviour.

The trial of Hamsun presented the prosecution with a difficult problem, – not because he was a famous author. Had he been 20 or 30 years younger, the verdict would have been clear-cut: indictment for treason, and a sentence of many years of imprisonment. Any other outcome would have been impossible if equality before the law should have applied. But Hamsun was 80 when Germany invaded Norway, 85 when the war ended. Could an 85 year old man be put in prison? Was it a matter of senility rather than treason? Would it be possible to dismiss the whole case? These were some of the questions that had to be considered, and opinions differ as to the decisions that were made. There would certainly have been criticism whatever the outcome.

During the deliberations about how to proceed against him, Hamsun had been placed in a home for the aged where he had considerable freedom of movement. Subsequently, the prosecuting authorities decided that, in view of his age, Hamsun should undergo a psychiatric examination. In their report the psychiatrists concluded that due both to his impaired hearing and his difficult relations with his family, Hamsun had lived very much in isolation during the war. As early as 1940, he had been suffering from arteriosclerosis, and in 1942 he had a cerebral haemorrhage which caused organic brain damage. One could therefore not exclude the possibility that his powers of resistance were weakened, making him easily influenced by others. Legally, they concluded, he should be regarded as a person of impaired mental capacity.

On the basis of the psychiatrists' report the Chief Public Prosecutor found that no public interest required the prosecution of Hamsun, who in addition to his impaired mental capacity was then 87 years old and practically deaf.

Nevertheless, he was brought to trial in a civil indemnities case, based on a clause in the Collaboration Enactment which made members of the NS collectively liable for torts. On 23 June 1948 Hamsun was sentenced by the Supreme Court to pay an indemnity of 325,000 kroner, his net wealth having first been assessed at just over 400,000 kroner. The verdict stressed Hamsun's particular responsibilities due to his position and authority as a world famous author. In his favour, his efforts on behalf of political prisoners, and his personal situation as assessed by the psychiatric report were emphasized. In assessing the indemnity, a major consideration was to leave Hamsun with sufficient means to live the rest of his life without financial worries.

With the clarity of hindsight, it may well be said that it would have been better if the case against Hamsun had been brought to court without a psychiatric examination, as he himself had wished. He felt the examination to be a severe personal humiliation, and was especially perturbed that the psychiatrists had persuaded his wife – herself an active member of the NS and very pro-German – to discuss their personal relationship. In a small book –

"On Overgrown Paths" – which he wrote in the old people's home at the age of 87, he mustered all his stylistic mastery to portray the psychiatrists and the treatment to which he had been subjected at the clinic in the worst possible light. Literary critics, taking the writer's side against the authorities, have often tended to accept this account as an objective description. In this way Hamsun got his revenge.

Hamsun's fate was a tragic one. But much of the criticism of the way he was treated after the war fails to allow for the situation at the time of the proceedings, when an attitude of bitterness against collaborators still prevailed. Critics of the proceedings also assume that genius should receive special treatment – an assumption that a state governed by law cannot condone.

THE TREND TOWARDS LENIENCY

It is presumably a common feature of judicial settlements, following a period of organised treason, that as conditions return to normal and the hostilities become a thing of the past, a psychological demand arises for having done with the affair and forgetting the wounds it has caused. This was indeed a noticeable feature in Norway after the war. There could be no question of any general amnesty; that would mean giving equal treatment to political seducers, dangerous criminal elements, and misguided youngsters. However, the institution of pardon was extensively used. The sentences passed during the first period after the liberation were systematically reviewed, and those that were found to be more severe than the level subsequently established were adjusted to that level by pardon. Provisions entailing a more lenient approach have also been adopted by statute. We have already mentioned the amendments to the Collaboration Enactment concerning the liability for torts which were introduced as early as August 1945. Some later statutory enactments of importance will be mentioned here.

An Act of 9 July 1948 provided that in future prisoners could be released on probation after having served one-half—instead of two-thirds—of their sentence. Some categories of offenders were excepted, such as profiteers, persons convicted of torture or other serious acts of corporal injury, and persons sentenced to imprisonment for more than eight years. The Act further provided that prison sentences of six months or less were to be commuted to suspended sentences, and that future prison sentences of that duration were also to be pronounced in the form of suspended sentences. This provision was based on the view that it would be pointless and undesirable to put people in prison for a few months on account of offences committed years ago, people who might by then have obtained work and found a place in the community.

Further modifications were contained in an Act of 28 July 1949. The Government proposal which led to the Act was intended in particular to cancel such loss of civil rights as had barred the offenders from opportunities to carry on a trade or obtain an education, for example the loss of the right to engage in business or handicraft, or the right to government employment. On the other hand, the proposal did not affect the loss of political rights, i. e. voting rights and the right to serve in the armed forces. However, the Storting took a further step and adopted a proposal providing that those who had not been sentenced to imprisonment for more than one year should also recover their political rights as from 8 May 1950, the fifth anniversary of the liberation, this date being chosen so as to emphasize that the Act was in the nature of an amnesty. From that date the minor offenders were thus legally reinstated as equal members of the community. Another Act of 22 May 1953 went further in the same direction, restoring most of the civil rights that had still not been recovered by that time.

THE PROBLEM OF SOCIAL
REHABILITATION

A settlement of this extent naturally gives rise to great human problems. All punishment means human suffering, both for those on whom the punishment is inflicted and for their families. But in the present-day view, the authorities must also assist the convict in finding a place in the community after his release. The problem of social rehabilitation was in this case a vast one, partly because of the large number of convicted persons, partly on account of the strong emotional atmosphere which surrounded the proceedings. The problem was highlighted by Sven Arntzen, the Chief Public Prosecutor, in a radio lecture on the proceedings given six months after the liberation. His lecture ended as follows: "And when the large number of persons involved have received their sentence and taken their punishment, we must re-admit them to the community, give them possibilities of employment and an opportunity to lead a normal life. We cannot let so many people remain apart to form an unhappy, discontented, anti-social population group." These words reflected the attitude of the responsible authorities, which was first opposed but later supported by public opinion.

There was much talk in the beginning of re-educating the collaborators. The purpose of the re-education was to make the offenders realize their own guilt, and to train them in the concepts of democracy. However, no serious and systematic effort was made to achieve this. It would have required numerous, highly qualified personnel in the prison camps, and an even greater problem would have been how to reach the many collaborators who were not in confinement. Even if all the material circumstances had been favourable, such an undertaking would have come up against great difficulties of a psychological kind. The political prisoner feels an intense emotional need to hear precisely those arguments that can relieve him of his guilt, exempt him from responsibility for the difficulties of his situation, and preferably turn him into a martyr of his convictions. And when many who are in the same situation can associate only with one another, their mutual influence will tend to create a system of concepts which may have little basis in reality, and which – because of the strong emotional involvement – makes them more or less immune to counter-arguments. It was commonly observed that shortly after the liberation most of the prisoners were willing to acknowledge their faults, but that this mood gave way later to a bitter and aggressive attitude. Those who admitted their guilt in court were liable to be ostracized by their fellow inmates when they returned to the camp.

Another problem, however, was more successfully solved than anybody had expected. Already at an early stage the authorities had clearly expressed the necessity of putting an end to the social boycott and of re-employing the collaborators. In the spring of 1946 an agreement was concluded between the Employers' Association and the Federation of Trade Unions which aimed at facilitating this process. The general shortage of labour contributed to a far better solution of the problem than had been anticipated. The Directorate of Labour had prepared special measures for providing NS members with work, but it proved unnecessary to put them into effect. Those who were released from the prison camps could as a rule find work straight away. A fact which perhaps contributed to this was that many of the prisoners while serving their sentences were engaged in agriculture, forestry and other outdoor work, some of them under conditions of considerable freedom. For the young collaborators, special prison camps were established for the purpose of providing them with the necessary vocational training.

The foregoing statements apply to the general run of collaborators. The problem proved more difficult for certain groups: those whose professions require a particular degree of confidence, especially clergymen, teachers, and lawyers. To restore them to their former occupations, if they had been guilty of serious offences, was a psychological impossibility. Many of them were elderly people who found it hard to start on a new course; to break with the past and embark on a new career requires indeed a combination of resignation and enterprise which many of them lacked. They became an unhappy and discontented, relatively small but intellectually well-equipped group, who have made it their prime purpose in life to find the weak points in the settlement with the collaborators and to discredit the proceedings in general.

Harder to answer than the question of employment is how NS members and other collaborators have been readmitted, in purely human terms, to the community. This process was no doubt more easily accomplished in rural areas, where the antagonism was not so pronounced as in the towns. Much has also depended on the attitude of the individual. Those who have taken an aggressive and defiant attitude have, of course, also had the greatest difficulties in being accepted.

In the winter of 1974 the discussion about social rehabilitation of collaborators had a strange sequel. The press disclosed that two of the new members elected to the Storting in the autumn of 1973 had been convicted of collaboration in their youth. One of them was 17 in 1945, the other 18. A sharp newspaper discussion followed, with strong demands that the two should withdraw from the Storting. However, they both withstood the pressure, and there was no legal basis for excluding them. One of them was reelected for a new term in 1977, and again in 1981.

Another revival of the debate occured in the winter of 1981, when the Norwegian State Broadcasting Corporation screened a TV series on the NS party, the years of occupation, and the post-war proceedings, presenting the views of the NS members themselves. Public response to the series showed that, more than 35 years after the end of the Occupation, the subject still aroused strong emotions.

THE CRITICISM OF THE PROCEEDINGS

The settlement with the enemy collaborators was an operation which has had such a profound effect on the nation's life that it has naturally given rise to controversy and debate. Much of the debate has taken place in a highly emotional atmosphere, which has given little scope for objective analysis and judgement. At first, the proceedings were mostly criticised for being too mild and insufficiently thorough. The labour press in particular complained that rich profiteers were able, with the help of good connections and clever lawyers, to delay their cases and conceal money and evidence. Gradually, the weight of criticism began to move in the opposite direction. Attention was called to the social consequences of making the proceedings too comprehensive, mitigating and extenuating circumstances were emphasized, legally doubtful points were brought up, and it was argued that the NS party's activities had come in for unduly concentrated censure, in contrast to other forms of unpatriotic conduct. Much of this criticism was of real value, and it was useful in that it tended to counteract the punitive mood which had at first dominated public opinion.

As time passed and the proceedings continued, however, another form of criticism began to assume greater proportions, criticism which did not aim at providing any objective analysis, but solely at rehabilitating the offenders by discrediting the judicial proceedings. The proceedings have been described as a form of political persecution of the unorthodox, accompanied by a cynical disregard of law and justice. A common version is that the proceedings were staged by the Nygaardsvold Government so that public attention could be diverted from the Government's own failings. Much of the propaganda took the form of violent attacks on the leaders of the resistance movement and on all who had played a prominent part in the proceedings. It even happened that German war criminals and Norwegian collaborators, while in prison, forged documents which were intended to prove that those who were playing a leading role in the proceedings had been German agents during the war. More common, however, is the use of war-time statements and documents which, quoted out of context and with a somewhat malicious intent, can be interpreted as expressing an unpatriotic attitude. The propaganda offensive also frequently includes fanciful accounts of ill-treatment and other misdeeds to which the prisoners have been exposed. An organisation called the "Federation for Social Rehabilitation" has been formed under the leadership of former NS members for the purpose of obtaining a review of the postwar proceedings against the collaborators. Outside their own circle hardly any support has been won for this idea.

In a few cases, the authorities reacted to these attacks by instituting criminal proceedings for libel. Thus, a man who, in a magazine he published, had accused the former Chief Public Prosecutor of acting as an informer during the war was sentenced in 1947 to nine months in prison for false accusation. But on the whole the authorities have refrained from taking legal action against the attacks.

It is sometimes argued that the post-war settlement has split the nation into two camps and opened up wounds which will take long to heal. But this argument confuses cause with effect. The split was created during the war, when a small part of the population chose to set themselves apart from the national community. Psychologically, the settlement has facilitated their return to the community. The argument that those who have taken their punishment have thus settled accounts with society and are entitled to another chance, has been of major importance in combatting social ostracism.

It may be noted that some Swedish nationals who had lived in Norway during the war, and who were sentenced by Norwegian courts for having assisted the Germans, got a private Swedish law institute *(Institutet för Offentlig och Internationell Rätt)* under the direction of Professor Sundberg at Uppsala, to write a paper on the legal proceedings in Norway, which was published in 1956. By its own statement, this publication was made possible by financial support from Norwegian citizens who had personally been convicted of collaboration. It strongly criticized the judicial proceedings on several counts, and concluded by stating that the clients of the Institute had been the victims of a denial of justice under international law. One of the clients applied to the Swedish Ministry of Foreign Affairs for assistance in having the judgement annulled for obtaining financial compensation. The application was refused. The Ministry of Foreign Affairs declared that the client had been convicted of assisting the enemy by manufacturing supplies intended for the occupying power. In the Ministry's opinion, there was no principle in international law which prohibited a state from inflicting punishment for acts of this nature, even when they have been committed by foreign nationals resident in the territory of that State. As for the allegation that the principle *nulla poena sine lege*—no punishment without law— had been disregarded, the Ministry observed that § 86 of the Norwegian Penal Code was in force already before the war and stipulates far heavier punishment for assistance to the enemy than had been inflicted in the client's case.

THE POST-WAR SETTLEMENT AND THE FUTURE

With a view the future, the Government in 1955 appointed a committee under the chairmanship of Supreme Court Justice Gundersen, a former Minister of Justice, for the purpose of collecting all the historical data on the post-war settlement with the collaborators. In 1962 the committee submitted a very extensive report, which is an inexhaustible source of information both on the actual events and on the debate which has taken place. In accordance with its terms of reference, the committee refrained from making any *appraisal* of the settlement. When the committee was appointed, the consensus was that no such appraisal could be made until the entire proceedings could be viewed from a historical perspective. Nor was it considered possible at the time to form a committee whose members would be sufficiently acquainted with the subject, without having, in one way or another, personally participated in the proceedings.

When in 1964 the Storting discussed the committee's report, the majority of the Storting Committee for Judicial Matters expressed the opinion that the settlements had on the whole been reasonable and just, and that there was no reason to open any new and general debate on the subject. This view is in accordance with the predominant opinion both in the Storting and in the nation as a whole. No doubt there are different opinions on this or that point, but the course which was followed may perhaps be said to represent a kind of average of the conflicting views. With time, it has apparently become a fairly widespread opinion that it would have been wiser to reduce the extent of the settlement, for example by omitting the prosecution of ordinary NS members. It is obvious, however, that this was not really feasible. No government would have been able in 1945 or 1946 to carry through an amnesty of NS party members.

The question may be raised whether the proceedings have served any purpose other than that of satisfying the popular demand for a just punishment of those who had broken the commandment of national solidarity.

It is always difficult to predict what lessons the future will draw from present-day events. Perhaps Norway will never again be exposed to aggression and war. We cannot know. We must be prepared for the possibility of having to face the same situation again, of seeing this country once more involved in a life and death struggle for its national independence and its free democratic government. Military preparedness is not enough. Experience has taught us to expect that both gold and political ideologies will be used for the purpose of undermining the population's solidarity and fighting spirit. In such a situation it is important that every citizen should understand that differences of political opinion are no excuse for stabbing the lawful authorities in the back while the country is at war. In the words of the Supreme Court, as it passed judgment on Quisling:

"In times and in circumstances of this nature, the requirement to each individual that he shall comply with the decisions of the lawful organs—the requirement of obedience and loyalty to those who lawfully represent the nation and the people—applies absolutely and unremittingly. When the nation's destiny is at stake, chaos must not prevail."

Literature

I. WAR COMES TO NORWAY

Norwegian neutrality in the 20th century:

Cf. O. Riste, *The Neutral Ally* (Oslo and London, 1965) for the First World War, and for the inter-war period N. Ørvik, *Sikkerhetspolitikken* 1920–39 (2 vols., Oslo, 1960/61). Concerning Britain, France and Scandinavia 1939–40, the main sources used are as follows:

British

Official Histories, Military Series:

BUTLER	Butler, J.R. M., *Grand Strategy*, Vol. II (September 1939–June 1941), London, 1957.
DERRY	Derry, T. K., *The Campaign in Norway*, London, 1952.
ROSKILL	Roskill, S. W., *The War at Sea*, Vol. I, London, 1954.

Official Histories, Civil Series:

	Medlicott, W. N., *The Economic Blockade*, Vol. I, London, 1952.
WOODWARD	Woodward, L., *British Foreign Policy in the Second World War*, London, 1962.

Memoirs, etc.:

CHURCHILL	Churchill, W. S., *The Second World War*, Vol. 1, Cassell, London, 1948.
IRONSIDE	Macleod and Kelly, *The Ironside Diaries 1937–1940*, London, 1962.

Regimental Histories:

Erskine, D. *The Scots Guards 1919–1955*, London, 1956.

Fitzgerald, D. J. L. *History of the Irish Guards in the Second World War*, Aldershot, 1949.

Hingston, W. *Never Give Up*. Vol. V. of *The History of the King's Own Yorkshire Light Infantry*, London, 1950.

French

GAMELIN   Gamelin, M. D., *Servir, Vol.* III (Paris, 1947).
MORDAL   Mordal, J., *La Campagne de Norvège* (Paris, 1949).
            Reynaud, P. *La France a sauvé l'Europe*, Vol. II
            (Paris, 1947). In addition, a motley collection of
            captured British and French documents from this
            period was published by the German Foreign
            Ministry as White Books 1940, No. 4 (Berlin, 1940)
            and 1939/41, No. 6 (Berlin, 1941).

            Norwegian policy in the period:
UK REPORT   *Undersøkelseskommisjonen av 1945, Innstilling I*
            (Report of the Parliamentary Commission of Inves-
            tigatian of 1945, No. I).
UK REPORT   *Bilag 1—8* (Appendices to the above-mentioned re-
APPENDICES port), Oslo, 1947.
            Koht H. *For Fred og Fridom i Krigstid* (Oslo,
            1957).

Statistics on the Narvik ore traffic can be found in:
    Karlbom, "Swedish iron ore exports to Germany 1933—1944",
    Scandinavian Economic History Review, Vol. XIII, No. I (1965),
    pp. 65—93.

The German plans.

For this topic a rich amount of documentary evidence is available.
The present account is based largely on contemporary records which
fall into two groups: first, German naval archives as printed in the
works listed below, and second, the diaries of centrally placed Germans such as Halder, the Chief of the German General Staff, Jodl,
Chief of Operations in OKW *(Oberkommando der Wehrmacht—*
Hitler's Supreme Command in name but in fact a co-ordinating staff
for the three services under the direction of Hitler as Supreme Commander of all German forces), and Rosenberg, the Nazi party's
"ideologist" and head of the *Aussenpolitisches Amt* or Foreign Policy
Bureau of the party. The chief sources to which reference is made
are as follows:

IMT   *The Trial of the Major War Criminals before the
            International Military Tribunal, Proceedings,*
            Vols. 1—23, and *Documents in Evidence,* Vols. 24—
            42 (Nürnberg, 1947—1949).

BRASSEY	"Führer Conferences on Naval Affairs 1939–1945", in *Brassey's Naval Annual 1948* (London, 1948), pp. 29–496.
HALDER	Halder, F., *Kriegstagebuch, Vol. I* (14 August 1939 –30 June 1940), Stuttgart, 1962.
JODL	(ed W. Hubatsch) Jodl's diary 13 October 1939– 30. January 1940, in *Die Welt als Geschichte* (Stuttgart) 1952, pp. 274–287 and 1953, pp. 58–71.
ROSENBERG	(ed. H-G. Seraphim), *Das politische Tagebuch Alfred Rosenbergs 1934/35 und 1939/40* (DVT Edition, München, 1964).

Accounts which include considerable documentary extracts:

HUBATSCH	Hubatsch, W., *Weserübung, Die deutsche Besetzung von Dänemark und Norwegen 1940* (2nd Ed., Göttingen, 1960).
GEMZELL	Gemzell, C-A, *Raeder, Hitler und Skandinavien* (Lund, 1965).

Other accounts:

SKODVIN	Skodvin, M., *Kampen om okkupasjonsstyret i Norge fram til 25. september 1940* (Oslo, 1956).
ZIEMKE	E. F. Ziemke, *The German Northern Theatre of Operations 1940-1945* (Department of the Army Pamphlet No. 20–271, Washington, D. C., 1959).
LOOCK	Loock, H-D., *Quisling, Rosenberg und Terboven* (Stuttgart 1970).

The Onslaught

For events in Norway on 8 April, see *UK Report* and *Appendices*. On 9 April and the war in Norway, see also the following accounts:

Norwegian: O. Lindbäck-Larsen, *Krigen i Norge 1940* (Oslo, 1965).

German: W. Hubatsch, *Weserübung* (Göttingen, 1960).

British: T. K. Derry, *The Campaign in Norway* (London, 1952) B. Ash, *Norway 1940* (London, 1964).

II. NORWAY UNDER OCCUPATION

For the first six months:

Undersøkelseskommisjonen av 1945, Innstilling and *Bilag*. (Oslo, 1947).

M. Skodvin, *Kampen om okkupasjonsstyret* (Oslo, 1956).

On resistance:

Th. Chr. Wyller, *Nyordning og Motstand* (Oslo, 1958).

S. Kjeldstadli, *Hjemmestyrkene* (Oslo, 1959).

See also Riste and Nøkleby, *Norway 1940–1945: The Resistance Movement,* in this series.

For the period as a whole:

Om landssvikoppgjøret (Oslo, 1962). (Report from a committee appointed by the Government to survey the proceedings against collaborators).

(ed. Sverre Steen), *Norges Krig,* Vols. I–III (Oslo, 1947–1950.)

III. NORWAY IN EXILE

The survey is based partly on unpublished documentary sources. The published sources include:

Norwegian

D o c u m e n t s:

Den Norske Regjerings Virksomhet under krigen fra 9. april 1940 til 22. juni 1945, Vols. I–IV (Oslo, 1948).

Innstilling fra Undersøkelseskommisjonen av 1945, I–VI (Oslo, 1946–47).

Bilag 1–9 til Innstilling . . . (Appendices to the preceding reports).

Regjeringen og Hjemmefronten under krigen (Oslo, 1948).

Utenriksdepartementet, *Norges forhold til Sverige under krigen 1940–45,* Vols. I–III (Oslo, 1947–49).

H i s t o r i c a l S t u d i e s:

O. Riste, *"London-regjeringa": Norge i krigsalliansen 1940–1945,* Vols. I–II (Oslo 1973–1979).

(ed. Sverre Steen), *Norges Krig 1940–45,* Vols. I–III (Oslo, 1947–50).

E. A. Steen, *Norges Sjøkrig 1940–1945,* Vols. I–VII (Oslo, 1954–).

M e m o i r s:

H. Koht, *For Fred og Fridom i Krigstid* (Oslo, 1957).

T. Lie, *Med England i Ildlinjen* (Oslo, 1956).

Ibid., *Hjemover* (Oslo, 1958).

British

O f f i c i a l H i s t o r i e s:

Grand Strategy, Vols. II (Butler); III, Part I (Gwyer) and Part II (Butler); V and VI (Ehrman). (London, 1956–64).

Civil Affairs and Military Government, Donnison, *North-West Europe* (London, 1961).

IV. THE POST-WAR PROCEEDINGS AGAINST ENEMY COLLABORATORS

Johs. Andenæs, *Det vanskelige oppgjøret* (Oslo, 1979).

Straffesak mot Vidkun Quisling (The Trial of Vidkun Quisling) (1946, 646 pp.) contains the shorthand records of the Quisling trial and the documents produced.

Om landssvikoppgjøret (On the Post-War Proceedings Against Enemy Collaborators). Report from a committee appointed to procure data for a report from the Ministry of Justice to the Storting (1962, 544 pp. plus appendices). The report provides a thorough survey of all matters relating to the settlement with the enemy collaborators, and the debate on the subject, with numerous references to other literature.

INDEX

(Italics refer to illustrations)

Jodl, General Alfred, Chief of Operations in OKW, 31, 34, 35, 36, 37, 41, 43.
"Jupiter", planned operation, 113.

Keitel, *Generaloberst* W., Head of OKW, 35, 39, 45.
Koht, Dr. Halvdan, Norwegian Foreign Minister, 46–47, 48, 56.
Kommissariske Statsråder, see Council of Commissioner Ministers.
Kristiansand, 35.

Lammers, Dr. H., Head of Hitler's Reich Chancellery, 72–73, 80.
League of Nations, 10.
Leningrad, 75.
Lie, Trygve, Norwegian Foreign Minister, 104, 106, 108.

Meidell, Birger, "Commissioner Minister", 84.
"Milorg", see Norwegian Military Resistance Organisation.
Mine-laying, in the First World War, 12, 14; plans and operations, 14–19, 22–26; in the approaches to Narvik, 47–48, 54.
Narvik, 14–41 *passim*, 44, 48, 53, 60, 61; mines laid in the approaches to, 47.
Nasjonal Samling (NS), 33, 34, 64, 67, 69, 70, 76, 80, 81, 88, 89, 122, 125, 131, 133, 150, 151, 152, 153, 154, 155, 156, 157, 160; controlled by *Reichskommissar*, 66; efforts to increase membership, 66–68; membership figures of, 70–73; and military co-operation, 74, 82, 83; and nazification in Norway, 70, 84, 86, 87; and the police, 76; mass arrests after liberation, 123–24; social boycott of members, 126; and assistance of the enemy, 133–37; and economic co-operation with enemy, 135–36; and the Collaboration Enactment, 140–44.
Netherlands, The, 32, 44, 61.
Neumann, *SS Obersturmbannführer*, 82, 83.
Norsk Hydro, 110.
North Sea, 11, 47, 106, 108; Mine barrage in First World War, 12; German invasion fleet in, 48.
Nortraship, Norwegian Shipping and Trade Mission, 98, 118.
Norway, prewar policies of, 9–14; Hitler orders occupation of, 41, 45; attacked by Germany, 49, 50; and state of war with Germany, 76–78, 80, 81, 137–39; liberation of, 99, 102, 103, 104, 112–14; restoration of economy of, 118.

Norwegian Air Force, 95, 101, 103, *103*, 104, 117, 120; and "Little Norway", Toronto, 100; duties, of, 100.
– Army, 38, *47*, 50–53, 95, 101, 102, 104, 117.
– collaborators, 140, 148; proceedings against after the war, 122–60; social boycott of, 126; and fines, 151; and loss of civil rights, 152; leniency towards, 153–54; rehabilitation of, 154–56; criticism of proceedings against, 156–59. See also *Nasjonal Samling* and Quisling.
– Constitution, 130, 132, 133, 135, 138, 142, 143; attacks on, 139–40.
– Defence Ministry in London, 109.
– Foreign Ministry during the invasion, 57.
– Government, 13, 20, 26, 35, 48, 54, 56, 57, 59, 63, 64, 68, 69, 81, 90, 99, 102, 104, 105, 109, 112, 120, 121, 124, 130, 138, 139, 147, 153, 157; protests to Allies, 17; and the *"Altmark* affair", 19; and mobilisation during the invasion, 50; leaves Oslo, 50; leaves Norway, 95, 96; issues Proclamation of 7 June 1940, 95–96; and the merchant navy, 98; and contribution to Allied war effort 98–102; deals with the scarcity of personnel, 100–101; and the Alliance, 102–107; supports post-war co-operation, 106–107; maintains contract with occupied Norway, 107–12; considers liberation, 113, 114; and agreement governing civil jurisdiction, 115–16; legislative powers of, 130–33; and the Collaboration Enactment, 141.
– High Command, 110, 112, 113; Capitulation Agreement signed by representative of, 95, 138.
– Justice, Ministry of, 87, 117.
– Legion, *73*, 75.
– Merchant Navy, 99, 101, 104; prewar size, 98.
– Military Resistance Organization ("Milorg"), 74, 83, *89*, 90, 110, 116, 117, 120, 122, 123; role in the liberation, 113–14, *119*, 120, 121; after liberation 124–25; and the Collaboration Enactment, 141.
– Navy, 18, 95, 101, *101*, 103, 117, 120; duties of, 99–100.
– Proclamation of 7 June 1940 (by the King and Government), 53, 77, 95–96, 138.
– Resistance, 64, 68–70, 79, 88, 90–91,